The Happiness in Child-Raising

I0121995

Tatsuo Yamamura / Hanns Stekel

The Happiness in Child-Raising

A Japanese-Austrian Project and Family Culture in Japan

PL ACADEMIC RESEARCH

Bibliographic Information published by the Deutsche Nationalbibliothek
The Deutsche Nationalbibliothek lists this publication in the Deutsche Nationalbibliografie; detailed bibliographic data is available in the internet at http://dnb.d-nb.de.

ISBN 978-3-631-66297-7 (Print)
E-ISBN 978-3-653-05530-6 (E-Book)
DOI 10.3726/978-3-653-05530-6

© Peter Lang GmbH
Internationaler Verlag der Wissenschaften
Frankfurt am Main 2016
All rights reserved.
PL Academic Research is an Imprint of Peter Lang GmbH.

Peter Lang – Frankfurt am Main · Bern · Bruxelles · New York · Oxford · Warszawa · Wien

All parts of this publication are protected by copyright. Any utilisation outside the strict limits of the copyright law, without the permission of the publisher, is forbidden and liable to prosecution. This applies in particular to reproductions, translations, microfilming, and storage and processing in electronic retrieval systems.

This publication has been peer reviewed.

www.peterlang.com

Contents

Dr. Hanns Stekel

Preface

This book is first and foremost a text written by Tatsuo Yamamura. For the English edition, we have added a description of a project developed by the Johann Sebastian Bach Music School in Vienna in cooperation with the author.[1]

During the course of this project, there were numerous opportunities for interaction, discussion, and deep thought which made it possible for us to gain a better understanding of the Japanese approach to teaching music and the overall education of children. Along the way, a number of open questions arose for which there was a strong desire to have answers.

One day, when the project was in a serious crisis due to the catastrophe in Fukushima, Tatsuo Yamamura presented this text, which he saw as an introduction to and an inspiration for teaching and learning,[2] a book intended to be given as a handbook to the parents of kindergarten and school children. We had previously attended lectures given by the author to parents in Japan, and thus were better able to understand what he hoped to achieve with this text.

The fact that a book about the day-to-day teaching of music in Japan has now become available to us in translation is remarkable enough. But, in addition, the author is not only a teacher of music, but also an expert in the field of education in general and a man with a great deal of experience. Both of these traits are perceptible in the lectures and make the book especially valuable for those of us who are not Japanese.

---

1   The Johann Sebastian Bach Music School in Vienna was founded in 2000 under the aegis of the Diakonie of the Austrian Lutheran Church. With almost 2000 students, it is one of the largest private music schools in Vienna. International exchange projects constitute a core component of the school's profile, alongside music programs carried out in cooperation with schools in the Lutheran school system, the promotion of music as a lifelong pursuit, and the preparation for university studies.

2   Tatsuo Yamamura.

The framework of this project continues to have an important influence because our music school learned a great deal during the years of its operation.

A primary insight is that international exchange programs in education should never operate simply on a superficial level; cultural exchange is not a marginal note, but rather it lies at the very heart of such undertakings. There is much to be gained from the sharing of knowledge and experience about how human beings learn and can be taught.

Cultural exchange only works when there is a true dialogue and when the strengths and unique characteristics not only of the other culture but also of one's own can be grasped.

This book is a landmark and also a guide for this and future projects.

Dr. Hanns Stekel
Vienna, April 2015

Tatsuo Yamamura

Overview for rising the initial issue on 50 Clues for Happiness

At some points, people would have been critics against education. And these critical words, against an educational revolution or a school revolution, could have been towards the abilities of teachers and the educational system itself by forcing responsibilities. They have yet to touch the things intentionally, despite many other important factors having a huge influence on children's learning. These are:

1) How much children have learnt from their parents.
2) If parents rouse eagerness for children to learn.
3) How often children have experiences towards self-learning at home.
4) How to face intercultural understanding at home.

These are the basic importance elements that must be taught at home with the interactions within family in order for children to obtain a certain result in their growth. There is a limitation where schools, kindergartens, or nursery schools have made enormous effort putting on behalf of their parents. To lead children to success or to have fostered children who have succeeded in their life, the imperative duty at home has to be mentioned without any hesitations. However, it is quite unfortunate that the people who are working in the educational field, such as teachers and also politicians, presumably have not mentioned anything about it.

The 50 clues written in the main content of this book are included to introduce one scholar's idea touched upon Japanese home education translated into English. The original is published in Japan under the title, *"Childcare theory for the age of convenience - Family culture and the cycle of happiness."*

As the central interest, the author has emphasised the importance of developing children's imagination in this book. Also, the author has understood an effect of the power of music in order to develop children's imagination by experience through the project that is touched upon later.

It is hoped that this book gives a clue to enrich the future of child rearing under a mutual culture by introducing the circumstances and the idea of Japanese home education as cultural exchange through the music that has given a mutual enrichment.

Introduction: Who is Responsible for Raising Children? Is it the parents or Society?

A while ago, an overwhelming majority would have said that the parents were responsible for raising children. In recent years, however, there have been increasing calls to hold society responsible for raising children, despite the fact that much better environments and resources are now available to parents for childcare than they were decades ago.

Granted, children grow up to form the core of that very society; therefore, calling the raising of children a social investment may, at first, sound logical. But I believe that the debate should focus on the family, the very bedrock on which people develop. Moreover, I think that child raising is not just about nice sounding catchphrases like "no scolding" or "not getting angry." Parents should make the most of all five senses and their sensibilities when raising their children. In that sense, I am confident of one thing: child raising, or being involved in any way with children for that matter, is the establishment of a lifestyle and culture of learning in the home. A happy side effect is that it leads to self-improvement and growth on the part of parents and other grown-ups.

Today's younger generations appear to be more self-centred than in previous ages. "Finding yourself" seems to be all the rage, and many youngsters spare no effort if it means that they can better themselves. I heartily recommend child raising and other child-related activities as an ideal way for today's self-interested youth to realise themselves. Parents enjoy learning from their children, who, in turn, have fun and learn as they watch their parents take pleasure in parenting; it is an endless loop of happiness where both parents and children have a positive influence on each other. Why else would humankind have kept up this process of child raising over millions of years?

We live in an age of information overload. Technological advances may have led to greater convenience, but the all-important work of child raising is in danger of being swallowed up by the wave of convenience. On the other hand, we are challenged by unprecedented events like natural disasters where we must sharpen our imagination and instincts to deal with these situations. In a sense, we must reconcile these two contrasting aspects of childcare when raising our children, but I think that the required fortitude will be nurtured within that loop of happiness.

The important thing is that parents learn from their experience, enjoy themselves, and evolve.

This book is based on the contents of a radio program, *Mako-talk!*, which was broadcast on FM Tochigi Radio Berry between March and December 2012, with some additions and editing. I served as an advisor on that program. The book gives examples of parents who, by merely changing their perspective, developed new insights and made discoveries that solved their child raising issues. I have also added comments based on my experience as a kindergarten principal and school counsellor. If you are a parent, you will have already discovered the joys of raising children long before you ever picked up this book. If you haven't, the book will hopefully help you make that precious discovery. If you are not yet a parent but may become one in the future, it will surely enhance your anticipation towards the experience of raising your children.

These days, many people avoid having, raising, and getting involved with children for all sorts of reasons, such as having no time, it being too much trouble, and it being too expensive. However, I can promise you that children will repay all investments of time and cost made by their parents and society many times over.

001: Growing Children Do as Their Parents Do, Not as They Say

Growing children do as their parents do, not as they say. Children are constantly watching their parents so no matter how much children are told to take their hands out of their pockets and stand up straight, they will continue to slouch around with their hands in their pockets if they see their parents doing the same.

No matter how much you coax them, children will never simply do as their parents tell them. However, they will always be influenced by what they see their parents doing; this is especially concerning because they see everything.

But why does this happen?

Children spend their first years under the close protection of their parents, during which time a strong bond is forged. However, at around two years of age, children begin to develop a sense of self and often want to do the opposite of what mum and dad say.

When children say that they don't want to, it is a sign that they are developing their own will that is separate from that of their parents. It is this independent will that stops children from simply doing whatever their parents say.

That said, children base the development of their cognitive selves on their parents, the people who are closest to them. For that reason, children constantly watch what their parents do, and parents' behaviour inevitably infiltrates that of their children. Therefore, parents would do well to understand how children develop their sense of self.

Recently, my son, now a university student, visited my kindergarten. "Don't slouch, boy!" I admonished him. Imagine my shock when one of my staff said, "He walks just like his father."

Could it be that our bodies memorise the behaviour of our parents as we observe them from childhood? This is quite possible and can happen more than we imagine.

In light of that incident, I now know that I need to keep an eye on my son's actions and attitude because they are a reflection of mine. Use your child's bad behaviour as a mirror by which to correct your own.

In that sense, your behaviour and movements as parents are a vital component of how you raise your children.

I believe that the fundamentals of good behaviour should be instilled physically through the insistence of basic manners at home, such as saying please and thank you. The primary means of achieving this is for parents to lead by example; it is much more effective for your children to see you saying please and thank you on a day-to-day basis than for you to nag them into doing so.

You may not realise it, but your children are constantly watching you.

002: Family Culture is More Useful Than "How to Raise Your Child" Books

Children do not come with manuals to explain to parents how to raise them. Certainly, there are many books on the market purporting to tell readers how to raise or discipline their children; however, there are no guarantees or data to say that following the advice in the book will ensure that you can raise your kids successfully. If raising children was a matter of following a manual, we'd all raise perfect children, but half the fun of the human experience lies in those areas where things don't go according to plan. In the end, our parents are our textbooks: If you absolutely must have a child raising manual, think about how your parents interacted with you.

Each child and each parent is unique, and each home has its own circumstances. As a result, there can't be a one-size-fits-all manual, and it is fine for each household to have its own standards and methods for disciplining children. The important thing is for each family to set its rules and enforce strict discipline when they are broken. After all, we all have to live within society's rules when we grow up.

There is one vital prerequisite for strict discipline: There must be an emotional attachment between the child and his or her parents. The progression from attachment into trust happens until the child reaches approximately three years of age; once that bond is in place, even scolding that may seem quite severe to an independent observer is not a problem between the parent and child in question because a foundation based on love has been established.

For that reason, I think it is important to hug your children or rub their backs after telling them off. Doing so cancels out the psychological distance that opens up between parent and child through the scolding. This repetition of distancing and closeness helps both the child and the parents to learn. Ultimately, raising a child is a process of growth for both parties.

Raising children is a trying business, but it can also be fun if you change your perspective. For instance, let's look at the parents who encourage their children to attend English lessons, karate school, or whatever because they want their kids to develop certain skills. That desire is based on the parents' own experiences and aspirations, rather than those of the children, so when the children inevitably lose interest and want to quit, the parents worry that the kids will fail to learn about the importance of perseverance and finishing what you started. I know this because I was one of those parents.

But that concern disappeared as soon as I actually tried learning the same lessons as my kids. Learning is challenging and also great fun. Maybe some of that enthusiasm rubs off on the children when they see their parents enjoying themselves. Seeing you set goals and work towards achieving them is, in itself, a learning experience for your children that gradually contributes to your own family culture, your original child raising manual.

003: Children Give a Lifetime's Worth of Love in Their First Three Years

"Children give a lifetime's dues in their first three years."

What a nice phrase. It comes from the book *Ano-ne, Daijobu, Daijobu* (*"Hey, It's Alright, It's Alright"*) by Fusae Yoshimaru (published by Chichi).

In the first three years of their lives, children are like little angels constantly hanging around their parents. This continual proximity awakens mothers and fathers to their role as parents and rewards them with the joys of loving and the inimitable wonders of a baby's laugh and smile. These memories can be treasured for the rest of your life, and that is why Yoshimaru said that children pay their parents a lifetime's worth of love" in their first three years.

Yet, as their children get older, parents tend to forget the lifetime of joy they received within those initial three years. Their aspirations for their children grow and begin to outweigh the memories of times past – mine certainly did. In fact, by the time their children reach university age, parents' perspectives have often reversed to the point where they think that their children are inconsiderate and uncaring.

Because of that reversal of perspective, some parents are put out to be told that children have already "paid their dues" with that lifetime's worth of joy in the first three years. It is certainly food for thought for parents of grown children.

Perhaps some parents will say that they missed out on those joys because their children were in day care all day. As a result, some mothers are indeed hesitant to leave their children in day care for long stretches. However, surely even children who attend kindergarten or nursery school "pay their dues" by being active and well behaved while they are away from home.

Meanwhile, children "paying their dues" is significant in another way. Having children enables parents to grow as people, and children are "paying their dues" simply by being children. Indeed, parents begin learning how to be parents in those first years. "Child raising is parent raising," as it were. Parents and their children grow up together, and therein lies the true meaning of the claim that "children give parents a lifetime's worth of joy in their first three years."

004: Read Picture Books for Your Own Enjoyment

One question I am often asked is: "What kind of picture books should I read to my child?"

Parents should, in principle, read books for their own enjoyment rather than just for the benefit of their children. In fact, the same goes for everything, not just picture books. If you read a book and don't enjoy it, chances are your children won't enjoy it when you read it to them. There may be times when children don't seem to be having much fun when you read them a book and they may even appear to be bored; however, it doesn't matter as long as you are moved when reading it. I believe that the sight of parents having fun is one of the building blocks of a family's culture.

What, then, should you be aware of when reading books to your children?

In my view, you should focus on reading *with* your children rather than *to* them. There is no need to put on voices for the different characters; leave that to professional narrators. Simply read the books aloud using your normal voice, just like you would read a newspaper. If you normally speak in a regional dialect, read the book in your normal, everyday accent. It's not the way you read that matters; the real significance lies in your children hearing your voice.

When a parent reads, their children imagine the story world unfolding in their minds as they listen, while the parents imagine what is going on in the children's minds. This process of sensing and imagining what the other is doing nurtures the bond between parents and children.

It is also important that you do not try to explain the picture books too much.

Take, for example, the Grimm Brothers' tale of *The Wolf and the Seven Young Kids*. In kindergarten, we had children make clay figures to depict scenes from the story. One time, a boy making the wolf declared that the wolf would smile. The other children rejected the idea. "Why would a wolf smile?" they demanded, "Wolves are supposed to be scary!"

When the teacher asked why he wanted to make a smiley wolf, the child replied, "He's happy, obviously, because he's going to eat the goats!"

His bemusement at the others' reaction stemmed from his lack of pre-conceptions: It turns out that he had never heard *The Wolf and the Seven Young Kids* before the teacher read it to the class. On the other hand, those children whose parents had read them the story at home insisted that the wolf was scary. Their image of the wolf was probably planted in their minds by their parents as they read the story.

It is fine for children to create mental pictures on their own as they listen to stories; the problem comes when parents plant pre-conceived images in their children's minds and foist their values onto the children. Such excessive parenting hinders the development of children's sense of self. Parents should not tell children that the wolf in the story is scary; the kids should develop and feel this for themselves.

You do not have to ask questions as you read them stories (i.e. "What do you think about this story?" or "What do you imagine the main character is thinking?"). That can wait until children start elementary school. Until then, parents should read picture books with their children purely for fun. By reading together, a priceless bond develops between parents and children that can only be created at that particular time of life. You don't want to miss out on it because of some misguided effort at development.

005: "He/She's Got to Think for Himself/Herself" Is Not Good for Your Kids

When children run into problems or are forced to make choices, many parents want the children to think for themselves; their first instinct is to foist the problem onto the children and say, "Sort it out for yourself."

Obviously, empowering children to think and choose for themselves is an important part of growing up; however, children are immature and inexperienced. Even when they do try to think for themselves, they will struggle to arrive at a solution unless their parents ultimately show them the end-point.

In this case, the "end-point" refers to the point at which the child can reasonably reach an acceptable solution to the issue at hand. The important thing here is that the child learns how to come to terms with a given situation.

That sounds complicated, but it's just a fancy way of saying "compromise." In life, it is important for us to develop a sense for what is a reasonable line and to say, "Oh well, I guess this will have to do." There are times when we put our views across even when we know that we have to yield some ground or that a solution can never be reached. In that sense, I think "Can't be helped" and "There's nothing else for it" are good phrases, and it is your job to teach them to your children.

The specific point of compromise will depend on the situation and even the individual family. But if parents have clearly defined principles, the judgment about where and when to compromise will not waver. Therefore, when your children come to you for advice, I hope you listen with sincerity and advise them based on consistent principles, such as that we must not cause trouble for others, that your suggested course of action is for the greater good, and that we should be honest and never sneaky.

006: Promises Without Action Are Meaningless

Let me tell you about an article I read in the Asahi Shimbun newspaper titled *Minna Egao de Iru Tame Ni (So that Everyone Can Be Happy)*. The article detailed the story of the headmaster of an elementary school in Osaka who made everyone promise that they would not do or say anything they wouldn't want others to do or say to them.

The most interesting point was that the promise was not just a promise; it led to specific action. Children who broke their "do unto others" promise would come to the headmaster's office on their own volition and confess their transgression. Anyone who was told to report to the headmaster by someone else had to "rewind" to the point in time immediately before the transgression took place and figure out for themselves how the incident might have been avoided.

The article made me wonder what parents are really doing when they repeatedly insist that their newly self-aware toddler or rebellious adolescent do what he or she is told. Perhaps they are actually just smothering their children's nascent ability to reject something that feels wrong to them. But this article showed me that it is important for children to be able to say "No!" when encountering a crisis of the mind.

In kindergarten, we encourage children to think about the promises they make to themselves during each particular activity. I believe that it is important, at school and at home, to make promises and guide children's behaviour towards keeping them. The problem lies in the lack of a link between promise and action; the educational goals we set at school or kindergarten, for instance, are forgotten and not used as a connection to specific behaviour.

Promises should not be just words; they should be a vehicle for developing actions and behaviour into positive habits. To achieve that, families need to turn promises into rules that children can adhere to. It may be neatly arranging your shoes when you come inside, it may be replacing things after you've used them, and it may be greeting everyone properly in the morning. The point is that you make sure that your children carry those actions out once the promise has been made. If, for instance, your child kicks off his or her shoes and leaves them in a mess by the door, call him or her back and make him or her arrange them properly; if he or she fails to put something back on the dining table that he or she was using, encourage him or her to put it away by saying, "None of us can eat dinner with the table in this state; it feels better if the place where you eat is clean and tidy." The important thing is that you make your child follow the house rules and keep his or her promises every day, no matter how bothersome it may be. It is vital that parents enforce these rules in their children from a young age. I hope that you will keep an eye on your childrens actions and behaviour as part of their daily routine at home.

007: Imagination is the Seed of Empathy

Have you ever thought about the difference between the words "kindness" and "empathy"? Kindness refers to thoughtfulness about tangible things, while the targets of empathy are intangible things. Mothers often talk about wanting to raise their children into considerate adults, but to do that, they need to develop their childrens ability to understand and sympathise with intangible things like feelings. In other words, they need to develop the skill of imagination.

The vital ingredient in developing an imagination is experience – lots of experience. Imagination is not a product of the head alone; it is based on past experience.

For instance, children know that just about everybody dislikes rain. In kindergarten, however, we want children to think about whether rain is actually unpleasant for absolutely everyone and, to that end, we have them observe the ecosystem of fireflies.

Fireflies lay their eggs in lakes and rivers. The eggs hatch and they develop into larvae underwater where they spend the autumn and winter growing until they are big enough to emerge onto land and burrow into the ground the following spring. There they make cocoons that they spend 60 to 70 days inside of before emerging as an adult firefly. One vital point in this development process is that the fireflies will only emerge from the water onto land on a rainy night. They never make the move to land on clear or cloudy nights.

It would be impossible for us to have children come and observe fireflies outside on a rainy night, so we made a film of the insects coming out of the water. Of course, the ideal situation would be for the children to see the fireflies flitting about in the dark, like stars in the sky, together with their parents. In fact, I once wrote a picture book, *One Philly's Exciting Night* (published by Zuisosha), about a father and son firefly who did just that.

Anyway, these activities teach the kids just how important water is to fireflies, and it pleases me to think that, instead of inducing disappointment, rain might inspire our children to imagine that tonight may be the night when the fireflies come out of the water and onto the land.

008: If You're Going to Discipline Your Child, Mean It

The line between disciplining your child and losing your temper at them is a much-discussed topic. Indeed, the internet is home to a lot of commentary on the subject. Some say that the difference is emotional. For example, that the act of discipline is reasoned, but if a parent lets emotion get the better of them, discipline crosses over to anger. Others say the difference is in who benefits. For example, venting anger benefits only yourself, while discipline benefits the child. Of course, there are cases where you start off disciplining your child and end up getting angry in the heat of the moment.

In any case, the general impression is that discipline is good and getting angry is bad. But I think that there is a place for anger, too. In fact, I believe that there comes a time as part of the child raising process when you have to show anger to your children and mean it. I would even go so far as to say that I think that shows of anger are one of a father's required roles.

There are, of course, cases where the father is absent for any number of reasons and the mother is left to maintain order as best as she can by using the unique skills at her disposal. In those situations, it is better to ask someone close to the family to take on the paternal disciplinary role than for the mother to shoulder that burden.

Anger is when you get emotional and your feelings are directed toward the target of your ire. From a parent's perspective, anger is an expression of your inner desire for your children to improve some facet of their person; additionally, it is unleashed when you are convinced that a show of anger is needed to stop your children from, for instance, doing something that will harm or trouble others. Anyone who has ever been the target of real, heartfelt anger even once recognises that they have reached the boundary of acceptable behaviour. Therefore, anger acts as a kind of brake that stops children from doing something that they must not do.

However, despite all of that, it is not about whether one is emotional or rational, or the difference between discipline and anger; the real issue here is the purpose and why you are angry. If you, as a parent, have a clear purpose in your anger, then distinctions about discipline and fury become irrelevant because your child will sense exactly what you are getting at.

If you notice that your children's behaviour is socially inappropriate, perhaps because it would cause trouble or discomfort for others if left unchecked, it is vital that you send your children a message. Having observed the situation at the front lines of the education community and seen the reports of crimes that have rocked society, I am convinced that the time is coming when families will be held responsible for the actions of their children.

009: Why is *the Cat That Lived a Million Times* so Popular?

The Cat that Lived a Million Times is a popular picture book, written by Yoko Sano and published by Kodansha, that can be found in virtually every kindergarten in Japan. Children read it, and most teachers and parents have read it, too.

But the book's popularity is a mystery to me. Don't get me wrong, I think that it is a fine book, but I wonder if children really enjoy this book.

It is about a cat that remains in a never-ending cycle of life, death, and rebirth.

In one of his lives, he is a king's pet; in another, he lives aboard a ship; in another life, he is a circus magician's cat. He lives and dies a million times, and every time he dies his owner is sad, but the cat is not sad because he hates each and every one of them. But in his millionth life, the cat is born a stray; no longer is he anyone's pet. He boasts about how he has lived a million times, and soon he is surrounded by admiring female cats.

But one cat remains unimpressed. He seeks the attention of the white female and gradually falls for her. Eventually, he proposes to her and they mate. The white cat bears him many kittens, but eventually she gets old and dies. For the first time in his million lives, the male cat feels sad and he cries a million times. Finally, he lies down next to his beloved white cat, dies, and is never reborn again.

This tale is unusual in that although the main character dies, the reader may think that it is a lovely story. Children are of course more likely to be sad that the poor cat died; in any event, their feelings are likely to be beyond their ability to express it in words.

I think that Yoko Sano has written a very profound story. The cat who had lived a million times within his own little world only begins to develop his conscious self when he becomes a stray and he only discovers the true value of living when he lets someone else into his life. The cat learns that

there is no point in living a million lives alone, but that there is real meaning in a single life lived together with another. *The Cat that Lived a Million
Times* is probably a story that is best appreciated once we have reached
our teenage years.

It can also be interpreted as a tale of achieving independence. The cat
goes from being someone's pet to being a stray and then, and only then, he
finds love and discovers the joy of letting others into his life. The message
is that life is not truly lived until you achieve independence, and surely the
same can be said for our children.

010: When It's Time to Make Your Child Give up on a Dream

Every year in March, we hold a graduation ceremony in kindergarten and
nursery school. These events typically end with the children announcing to
the assembly what they want to be when they grow up before proceeding
out of the auditorium for the last time. Some children want to be astronauts,
some want to be the ice cream man, some want to own a cake shop, some
want to be violinists, some want to be police officers, and so on. Listening
to them makes me want to give them a big round of encouraging applause.

Children sometimes have secret dreams about what they want to be, and
how they want to be, in the future. It is important that they are able to hold
on to these dreams, in private if they desire. Maybe they think that their
vision will be laughed at or rejected, so they protect their aspirations by
keeping them to themselves. I see great strength of will in that act, which
shows just how much those dreams mean to the children.

However, not every parent can make their child's dreams come true. The
father of Ichiro Suzuki, one of Japan's biggest baseball stars and latterly a
regular fixture of Major League Baseball, not only picked up his boy from
school every day and took him to a batting cage to practice, but also in-
vested huge sums of money in his son's future. That kind of dedication is,
however, beyond the means or capacities of most parents.

Most importantly, parents need to be there when a child must give up a
cherished dream. When there is absolutely no hope of achievement, I think
that parents need to help their children give up on their dream.

For instance, I have twin sons and one of them had long hoped to be a
baseball player when he grew up, from his earliest years. He duly joined

his high school baseball team, but gradually became emotionally unstable after a period of time.

He had tried so hard to earn a regular spot on the starting line-up, but it seems that trying too hard for too long makes the heart brittle. His 30-minute commute was haunted with doubt: "Why am I not good enough? Why can't I make the starting line-up?"

When I realised my boy was in a crisis, I decided I had to relieve his suffering. Naturally, he was against the idea of quitting the team. Perhaps he was also concerned for the teacher who coached them, too. That was all the more reason why I, as his parent, had to step up to the plate.

I believe that parents must make judgments about whether a child is in crisis because they are the ones with a close-up view of the situation. Equally, however, the parent who convinces their child to give up a dream must take responsibility for it. "I know you wanted to keep up with it, son. I encouraged you to give up. I said it would be all right, don't worry."

It is vital that you take the burden of responsibility off your child's shoulders with words like these. I am convinced that making momentous decisions like those are a father's job.

011: The Valuable Lessons of Risk

Many parents take their children into the great outdoors in the summer holidays to encourage them to observe nature. Sports and other outdoor activities provide the ideal chance for fathers to get involved.

One popular activity in Japan is beetle hunting. Beetles are hard to find and catch, but that makes it all the more joyful when you succeed. Maybe you have smothered nectar on a tree in the evening hoping to lure beetles the next morning, only to find out come daybreak that you've attracted longicorns and moths but no beetles. Even worse, you may have caught the attention of dangerous wasps or hornets. But that is the point, it's no use not doing anything outdoors because there are dangers; teaching children how to get along with Mother Nature, dangers and all, is part of a father's job description.

These days, kindergartens and elementary schools are wary of doing anything that involves risk, even if they know that it would be a good experience for the children. For instance, sharpening pencils with a knife is a good way to train children to use their hands deftly, but schools are loath to let children wield a knife for fear that they might hurt themselves.

In this case, the onus of giving children beneficial experiences that may be slightly risky falls on parents. I believe it is the job of the father to support this. For example, when supervising your children's first times riding a bicycle without training wheels, tell them, "It's okay, I'm watching you. I'll make sure you don't fall."

Another example is bonfires. I love bonfires, and when I worked part-time at a parking lot as a teenager, we often had bonfires in the autumn. It is unfortunate that people have fewer opportunities to enjoy bonfires these days because of environmental concerns. I think that lighting a fire is a life skill that should be passed from parent to child. That's why I run for people with disabilities any time I use a flame as part of my activities in kindergarten or the facility; I try to have the children help me light it whenever it's possible.

Bonfires give us the pleasure of warmth but also teach us a fear of fire. I remember when I was young, helping the grown-ups on the farm, my uncle lit a bonfire to burn grass clippings but the fire caught on to dry grass alongside the nearby railway lines. My uncle and I worked frantically and somehow managed to put it out, but only just. In this way, I learned the dangers of fire through this experience accompanied by an adult.

Fear of danger is a necessary part of life and it is an important lesson. In that sense, it is a good thing to let children experience bonfires. Fire is indeed a mysterious element: Of course a crackling fire warms our hearts, but handling it unsettles us. If you have a chance, I highly recommend experiencing a bonfire with your children.

012: Teaching Perseverance Needs a Purpose

Now, more than ever, we need to foster the ability to accept adversity and bear disappointment when things don't go as desired. Children who are quick to temper lack this patience and, when I look at kindergartens and nursery schools today, I see that they are not successfully instilling this quality in their children. The root of the problem surely lies in the spoiling of children at home. Perhaps the thing I would encourage you to do above anything else is to ensure that you discipline your children in a way that develops their ability to accept it quietly when they don't always get their way.

For our part, kindergartens and nursery schools will invest considerable effort into teaching children how to get along comfortably with each other in a communal situation while still making the most of their individuality. Naturally, this means that everyone will need to compromise, but instilling perseverance is not our main focus; amid this correlation between group and individual, our aim is to teach children how to live in harmony with others. The group interaction of kindergarten is the vehicle through which we aim to develop children's ability to control their own behaviour.

Children are fascinating in that respect. For instance, in my kindergarten, there is a narrow ledge above a landing in an internal staircase for cleaning a high window, and the children get a thrill from climbing up and playing there. We told them many times not to, but they'd still do it. Then, one day, we put up a sign saying, "Is it okay to play here?" and, all of a sudden, they stopped. In this case, the children kept each other's behaviour in check through mutual agreement on what they could and couldn't do.

As you can see, group life in kindergarten is not primarily about teaching children to "live with it" when they are told not to do something they want to do (i.e. refraining from playing in a particular place), but rather develops the ability to think about their behaviour. In this case, it led the children to reach a decision among themselves that they should not play on the ledge because it was dangerous. Certainly, that ability is based on controlling one's desires, but this is not something that can simply be taught in kindergarten. Perseverance is one of the most fundamental human skills that needs to be taught at home and not in the community.

To instil in children the patience to accept that some things won't go their way, each home needs to make and enforce rules. For example, I am sure that many homes do not allow family members to watch television while eating. Adhering to that rule is an act of perseverance.

The important thing is that the grown-ups of the house comply with the rules they set for their children. There is no way you can expect your children to refrain from watching television while eating if you do it yourself. Rules are only rules for children when they apply to parents as well.

Making rules enforces patience. That is why I encourage mothers to make rules at home intended to instil this quality in their children. After all, it is the children themselves who will suffer when they enter kindergarten or nursery school, and when they grow up and enter the workforce, if they have not learned how to control themselves when things don't always go their way. For instance, some children still feel compelled to bring their toys to kindergarten when they should have learned long ago at home to do without them.

On the other hand, parents should respect their children's wishes as much as possible, just as long as they don't spoil them. My experience leads me to believe that children whose wishes are respected when appropriate also know when it is appropriate to accept being told "no" and can handle their disappointment when required.

013: Einstein's Views on Imagination

Albert Einstein is one of my favourite heroes. I particularly like that famous picture of him poking his tongue out; his expression is wonderfully mischievous. I admire the way he actively sought answers to his childhood questions like, "Why is the sky blue?" and "Why is the sun orange?" He did not make typical excuses like, "That's just common sense," or "It's always been that way." When Einstein had a query, he set about finding a solution.

My favourite Einstein quote is:

> "I am enough of an artist to draw freely upon my imagination. Imagination is more important than knowledge. Knowledge is limited. Imagination encircles the world."

Einstein said that imagination was everything. That reminds me: I once read that the two things humans gained from the evolutionary process were imagination and language. In other words, when chimpanzees and humans parted ways at the fork in the road of evolution, the chimps retained their eidetic memory, while humans ditched that skill and acquired the ability to imagine and speak. That, I suppose, is why we are able to communicate our thoughts and take action to realise our dreams.

So how do people nurture their ability to imagine? I believe the most important factor is the wealth of childhood experience, particularly during the toddler years. Obviously experiences need to be balanced and children should not become too stilted in any one direction, but the important thing is that children are exposed to a variety of different things, whether it be music, art, or something else. Some people believe that English should be the only early education provided, while others think that there is no need for formal schooling in the early years and that children should just run around and play outside at this stage. Both of these views are extremes.

Early childhood experiences are our bedrock; they are the basis of our imaginative abilities and pave the way for children to grow into individual adults with unique personalities. To narrow the scope of a child's seminal landscape is to narrow the development of his or her imagination and personality in later life.

Early childhood is a vulnerable time, but it is also when children learn to imagine and believe in their imagination. Though, as they grow older, children seem to lose interest in their former passions, such as drawing pictures or listening to fairy tales. As teenagers, children who once loved to walk hand-in-hand with their parents wouldn't be caught dead holding hands with mum or dad. At first glance, it looks like they have lost their imagination and it makes us sad, but this process may in fact be the evolution of imaginative ability. I believe that a rich imagination bolsters children through puberty in their own unique ways.

What is more, I also think that many of our social problems are caused by a lack of imagination, which in turn is caused by a dearth of experience in early childhood. In that sense, it is vitally important for children to experience many things in their early years.

Let me finish this chapter with two heart-warming stories about how imagination changed a child's situation for the better.

The first concerns a three-year-old boy in kindergarten who refused to eat his school lunch. We didn't force him to eat, thinking that he would gradually come around. Then one day, one of the teachers said, "You know, that's the rice your grandfather worked so hard to make on his farm," and it was like a switch went on in the boy's mind. All of a sudden he began to eat. I suppose he already had vague images in his head about life with his grandfather and his grandfather's hard work, and that one comment showed him how to connect these two things, A and B. At that instant, you could almost feel the boy grow.

The second story concerns my daughter. One day when she was about eight years old, she came home from school and laughingly told us, "Just like last year, I'm on toilet cleaning duty again. Not only that, I am responsible for cleaning the toilet bowls, not just the taps and sinks like last year."

I really wondered what was going on in her mind, but just said, "Wow, that's great. It's similar to that song you love, *The Toilet Goddess*. How does it go? Something about 'if you work hard to keep the toilet clean the toilet goddess will smile on you and you'll be blessed with good fortune.' Good for you."

My daughter began to recall the lyrics to the song. The moral of this story is that when children encounter something that challenges their values (in my daughter's case, she had probably been thinking, or maybe her friends had told her, what a terrible thing it was to be on toilet cleaning duty), a little appropriate advice and a broad imagination can empower children to change their perspective and move on to the next stage of development.

I guess Einstein was right.

014: Why We Teach Children About Air

Life is just as much about the little things as the major things. All of those insignificant things that we do unthinkingly, like working up a thirst, blinking in the sunlight filtering through the leaves, remembering an old song, and even sneezing, are part of the jigsaw of life. Ironically, the most fundamental aspect of life is so obvious that we hardly ever think about it: I'm talking about breathing.

When my wife was in labour with our youngest daughter, I was surprised to be summoned by the nurse into the delivery room to witness the birth. I will never forget my baby daughter's first cries. Obvious though it may seem, I was struck by the fact that breathing comes before all else, even crying. It is the first real act of life. At that moment, I was hit with the realisation that breathing air is integral to life. And yet, we take air and breathing for granted and don't think about its importance.

In kindergarten, we occasionally use experiments to teach the children about air and how amazing it is that humans are constantly breathing in and out without really thinking about it. For instance, we make hot air balloons out of trash bags to show that although air appears to be weightless, it actually has weight. In this way, we like to encourage children to re-examine their preconceptions about things that seem obvious at first glance.

015: Children See Through Grown-up Mendacity

Owen is a storybook by Kevin Henkes that I recommend to every grown-up. If you have only read it as a child, read it again as an adult because I am sure that you will make new discoveries.

The book is about a boy mouse called Owen who carries his yellow blanket, called Fuzzy, with him everywhere he goes. The blanket is dirty with food stains and Owen's mother and father are ashamed that he would carry such a thing around with him. They try to take it from him but Owen thinks up ingenious ways of thwarting them. The battle runs on for ages before one-day, Owen's mother has an idea: Instead of taking Fuzzy away from Owen, she finds a way to turn the blanket into something Owen could carry around with him.

This is a lovely story about how parents can resolve problems while taking their children's feelings into account. Many children are attached to something that brings them comfort, such as a blanket, stuffed toy, or other object. The most interesting point of *Owen* is that the young mouse was able to foil his parent's efforts to take Fuzzy away from him. In other words, children can see right through adult behaviour, and Owen makes it painfully clear that grown-up tricks that miss the point will not work on children.

The story ends with Owen's mother coming up with an idea so that Owen can keep Fuzzy with him all the time; she gives up on trying to take it away and instead turns it into a handkerchief so that he can always carry it around. She realises the importance of accepting her child's feelings rather than forcibly stealing away something that he loves.

The main message of this book is clear: Child raising is not just about changing your child to suit your tastes; parents need to be able to change their own perspectives, too.

Reading *Owen* reminded me of the Serenity Prayer by American theologian Reinhold Niebuhr.

"God, grant me the serenity to accept the things I cannot change, the courage to change the things I can, and the wisdom to know the difference."

It seems to me that Owen's mother used her wisdom to guide her son to independence rather than fighting him. From a parent's point of view, it may be easiest to just take the blanket away from your child, but the child's feelings will inevitably be injured. It is important to find a solution that accommodates your child's feelings. There are no black-and-white or right-and-wrong answers in child raising; it takes imagination and creativity.

016: What Happens When You Don't Discipline Your Children

These days, we hear a lot about child raising methods that avoid any scolding. Quite frankly, I find it disturbing not to chasten a child when he or she has done something wrong. People are, after all, animals of emotion, and we live in an environment where we experience a range of emotions that form the fabric of life. This encourages personal growth for both children and parents. Humans have multiple emotions because we need all of them, and anger is no exception. So it is unnatural to withhold anger when it is called for, and parents should not be so foolish.

Even those parents who absolutely refuse to admonish their children will surely agree that some degree of discipline is necessary. The process of disciplining and being disciplined instils each family's unique values and culture in each child and reinforces family ties.

Praise and affirmation alone do not build children's trust in people. Kids must also be exposed to discipline, anger, and sorrow in order to grow. Experiencing emotional discomfort such as being disciplined or scolded, being taught a sharp lesson, and being monitored for progress are just as important in building trust as praise and affirmation.

Having said that, I think that we need to be wise in how we discipline children these days. Before scolding a child or allowing yourself to show anger, pause, take a deep breath, and once you begin, make sure you are careful, relaxed, and not over-emotional. Some parents want to be their children's buddies, and there's nothing wrong with being a parent that is easy to relate to; however, there are times when you have to be the adult and take on the role of a tough teacher.

Think about why we even raise children. Our purpose is not to become friends with our kids; it is to prepare them to make their way in the world. In past ages, educators used phrases like "tough love" and "strictness is kindness" to show that children need a healthy mix of discipline and tenderness. Today, we have a slightly different worldview, but readers will surely agree that traditional Japanese families had a fine balance of those two aspects with the stern father and the gentle mother. I believe that discipline and anger are necessary in order to provide our children with an opportunity to experience that vital element of strictness.

017: How to Raise Your Children to Stand up to Bullies

Bullying is a concern for all parents; any child may be affected which means no parent can ignore the issue. No one wants his or her child to have any part of bullying, whether it is as the bully, the victim, or the passive on-looker. What, then, can you do?

I think that the solution starts at home by giving children clear guidelines on acceptable and unacceptable behaviour. Teach your children to not do to others what they would not want done to them, to not tell lies, and to respect all things, both animate and inanimate. These are very simple lessons to teach, but the important thing is that you provide your child with consistent guidance from early childhood.

When I take my elementary-school-aged daughter to the bus stop every morning, I always tell her two things: have fun at school and watch out for cars. That's it, nothing else. I am convinced that the real value in those messages is in the constant repetition. Whatever your message, if you repeat it often enough, it will seep into your child's mind and one day begin to act as an inner voice that becomes a guiding force. It is a curious thing: When a child is tempted to take that first puff of a cigarette, it is the sound of their parent's voice inside his or her head that will caution them against smoking.

Another effective means of developing a moral compass is to continually remind children from a young age that someone is always watching them when they do something naughty, whether it be God or the heavens or whoever else.

Let me share two episodes that illustrate this effect. Once, when my son was around kindergarten age, he was playing with his friends when one of them moved to steal one of my son's cards. My boy noticed what was happening and told his friend, "The police will catch you if you do stuff like that." Then, around the time he was in his fifth year of elementary school, I had him make a sand tray as a form of sandplay therapy (as a budding educational researcher, I wanted to observe the psychology of my twin boys). I was interested to note that, despite having very different personalities, both boys included police stations in their sand trays. It struck me then that repeated warnings that they must not be naughty or that they would get into trouble with the authorities had formed a deep-set awareness of right and wrong in their minds.

My point is that repeating important lessons offers children vital guidance for proper behaviour. Words that are constantly reinforced become the tenets that they live by and the weapons that they defend themselves with. If there is something you believe is important for your children to know and live by, you must reinforce it often.

018: Look Within Yourself for the Root Cause

Look at a standard map of Japan and it will appear bow-shaped, with Hokkaido at the top and describing a downward crescent. But what if you viewed Japan from a different point, for instance, from Europe? Our country would appear horizontal rather than vertical, with Kanazawa in Ishikawa Prefecture at the approximate centre. I refer, of course, to differences of perspective; changing your perspective can be very effective in everyday life, too.

Take, for instance, Japan's so-called "May blues." In kindergartens, schools, and workplaces nationwide, the new fiscal and education year starts in April, and after the initial euphoria of encountering a new environment, fatigue and difficulties kick in after about a month. Many children (and parents) succumb to this malaise. When their child says that they don't want to go to kindergarten anymore or that they fought with a classmate, many parents are quick to lay the blame on the teachers or their child's foe. But it's not always that simple.

I remember we once had a child in kindergarten who threw a tantrum every morning at the school gates and cried to go home. At first, we couldn't figure out why, assuming that he was just being selfish or going through a rebellious phase. But eventually we learned the real reason which was something far beyond anything we had imagined. Apparently, the boy's parents had begun divorce proceedings. They had tried to keep it secret from him but he had worked out what was going on. So, he cried every morning because he was afraid his parents would disappear while he was at kindergarten. As I have said before in this book, children see and notice much more than you realise.

This example shows that when the children are experiencing issues, parents tend to look for outside causes, although the actual reason often lies within the family relationship, most commonly involving the parents themselves.

We should probably not be so quick to blame others or lay problems at their feet when trouble arises. Instead, we should first examine the issue from a different perspective to see if we ourselves may not be the problem.

Searching for the cause of a problem within yourself can be unpleasant, but you should be brave and do it for the sake of your children. Avoid preconceptions and employ a fresh perspective which may lead you to the awful realisation that you were the cause of your child's problem. That should be a small price to pay if it subsequently benefits your child's development.

019: Bargaining With Your Children

Children, it seems, are always asking for one thing or another, such as the latest toys, game cards, consoles, etc. There is always something. Parents typically make a decision about whether or not their child really needs what they are asking for and buy those deemed necessary. If you ask me, though, this is a wasted opportunity. If you're going to buy them the necessities anyway, it is better to turn it into a bargain situation where children receive those things in exchange for doing chores, such as helping their parents around the house, cleaning up, or other jobs within their ability to perform.

This lesson is well illustrated in the story *Pelle's New Suit* by Elsa Beskow. It is a story of a young shepherd boy called Pelle who grows out of his clothes as he becomes older. Pelle shears one of his sheep and has the wool spun, dyed, woven into fabric, and made into a suit. Finally, he says thank you to the sheep.

Interestingly, when Pelle asks his grandmother and mother to spin the wool into yarn, they bargain with him, saying that they will do it only if Pelle helps them with work around the house. Pelle is a good, sincere boy, and agrees to help his grandmother and mother in exchange for the spun yarn. Throughout the book, Pelle asks different people for help in getting his suit made and enters into bargains where he works for his reward. I think that it is a wonderful story that teaches readers the value of hard work.

While it is important for parents to respect their children's wishes and requests, setting conditions that the children work for them (providing, of course, that the chores are within the children's capabilities) teaches the children that they can achieve their goals and get things that they want through their own efforts, and that those rewards are often sweeter when you actually earn them.

I recommend this kind of bargaining when raising your children. The best conditions are those that the child can achieve with little effort, such as running errands or clearing away the dishes after meals. The experience of getting what you want through work is highly beneficial to children's development. Moreover, linking their wishes or requests with work by making them perform tasks stimulates their brains, as does work that involves using their hands and fingers; it's not for nothing that our fingers are often referred to as our "other brains." In that sense, making your child work for something can have a profound beneficial influence on their development.

020: The Rise of Visually Focused People

I sometimes lecture at university. The students, rather than listening to what I'm saying, seem to spend more energy copying down my PowerPoint slides and lecture notes. I get the feeling that there are more "visually focused people" these days. Perhaps that's not surprising given the influence of television and video games. Visual people believe that they have understood something at first glance, but they struggle to explain things in words, which suggests to me that visual stimulation does not automatically lead to the ability to understand things logically.

It is said that newborn babies quickly acquire the ability to recognise things visually. Apparently, their range of sight extends around 30 centimetres, so a baby is able to discern its mother's face when breastfeeding. In that sense, you could say that people are visual animals from the time that they are born. As babies begin to crawl, their view of the world changes and their perspective becomes exponentially larger when they begin to walk at around one year of age.

For that reason, children should be given plenty of opportunities to watch things that visually stimulate their brains up to their preteen years. However, logical understanding of the things that they see requires a different kind of training. In my view, the cause of today's prevalence of highly immature university students is a lack of this kind of training. For instance, I have seen students examine a leaf under a microscope and all they can say is, "Wow, that's pretty." They lack the vocabulary to adequately describe what they are seeing.

While an emphasis on visual stimulation is fine in early childhood, when language and logical abilities have yet to be developed, children will need to grow out of that phase at some point. In addition to visual capabilities, it is vital that the abilities to feel, to express in language, and listen are developed. In my opinion, all those skills combined equals imagination.

Television and video games require no imagination and fail to stimulate the brain. You literally just watch them.

Conversely, observing nature does stimulate the brain. Rachel Carson, who wrote *A Sense of Wonder*, has spoken about the importance of parents exploring nature together with children. You don't have to consciously teach your children anything; just looking is fine. The point is that you look and are amazed together. This experience leads to the development of a sense of wonder.

Is it my involvement with young children as a kindergarten principal that makes me despair at these university students who are more concerned with taking notes than actually listening to what's being said and forces me to wonder what kind of early childhood they had. I doubt it; I am sure that all parents would look at these students and shake their heads.

021: The Time I Smacked My Kids and Meant It

Let me tell you about the time when I became truly enraged and yelled out loud while disciplining my child.

When my son was in the sixth year of elementary school, he scribbled all over the pencil case of a girl in his class, ruining it. I found out about the incident when I got home from work that evening and immediately made him call the family and apologise. And then, excessive though it may seem, I gave him a good, hard punch. These days, that might be called child abuse.

At the time, though, my only thought was that my son needed to learn a painful lesson; failure to put a stop to such behaviour then and there would surely lead to trouble in his future.

Later that night, my son, accompanied by his mother, went to the girl's house to apologise in person.

My hope is that my son will recall this experience when he grows up and that it will renew his dedication to becoming a good person. In fact, I think it is a parent's responsibility to provide these salutary lessons.

I was deliberate in my show of rage, telling myself to make the fire and brimstone count, knowing full well how awful we would both feel afterwards.

As you may expect, there was inevitably a cooling of parent-child relations afterwards. I felt uncomfortable and there was a distinct chill in the air. But those effects are only temporary, and that kind of discipline is necessary in the long run. When you discipline your child, I think that it is important that your anger be backed by the full weight of your convictions and your determination to raise your child as an upstanding citizen. It is up to each family to work out the boundaries between appropriate and inappropriate anger because each household has its own circumstances and every parent and child is a unique individual. There is no one-size-fits-all manual for childcare.

022: Family Culture

Many things happen within a family; sometimes, it seems, there are more downs than ups. Each family develops its own unique culture as it deals with the events of daily life. I believe that family culture is important because it provides direction for children throughout their lives and is handed down to subsequent generations.

Family culture is a central theme of *In America*, a wonderful movie that tells the tale of Johnny, a struggling actor, and his family, comprised of his wife Sarah and their two young daughters Christy and Ariel. The young Irish family moves to a rundown tenement in Harlem to begin a new life. Despite being poor, they try to make the most of their new life in New York. However, Johnny and Sarah labour under the crushing sadness of the death of their young son Frankie. Johnny finds night work as a taxi driver to pay for his daughters' school fees, and Sarah discovers that she is pregnant.

One Halloween, the daughters meet Mateo, a Nigerian artist who lives in the same building, and he becomes a family friend. Mateo has Acquired Immune Deficiency Syndrome (AIDS) and gradually grows weak throughout the movie. Meanwhile, Sarah's baby is born prematurely and perilously weak. Mateo finally succumbs to his illness on his bed at home, but at that very moment, Johnny and Sarah's baby shows signs of a healthy recovery and lets out a cry of terrific strength. It is a miracle that renews this family's hope for the future.

The grief and guilt of Frankie's death weighs heavily on the family. The two girls feel a bond with their lost little brother in their own ways, while the parents blame themselves for his death. As Mateo's spirit leaves his body and ascends unseen to heaven against a full moon sky, Ariel asks him to take care of Frankie and waves him farewell. Sharing her burden with the unseen but keenly felt spirit alleviates Ariel's sadness of losing her brother. It is a moving scene that suggests that sharing our burdens with others lightens our load, and it struck me that such fraternity is an important part of everyone's quest to realise their hopes and aspirations.

Finally, there is a moving speech from Christy, who had been a minor character to that point, who tells them how she held the family together. When the grief of Frankie's death threatened to overwhelm Johnny and Sarah, it was Christy's playful personality that encouraged them to carry on.

023: Be a Father, Not a Buddy

Fathers used to be imposing and inspired both fear and respect in children. These days however, they are merely kind and gentle, and it is almost as if they are buddies with their kids. This is unfortunate because fathers must not be their children's friends. Let me explain...

I believe that every family needs a father figure who fulfils all aspects of the paternal role (language, attitude, and expressions). For instance, if a child causes a problem, perhaps someone gets hurt, the father needs to lay down the law: "This is your fault. Go and apologise."

On the other side, after hearing a sincere apology, the father of the injured party should defuse the situation and say, "This issue is done. Let's move forward." A father should be principled and gracious, with the capacity to take everything into perspective and reach a reasonable conclusion.

Unfortunately, that is not always the case nowadays. We hear of children whose apologies are met by irate fathers who threaten legal action. This kind of reaction serves only to destroy all relationships.

I believe that this trend stems from the father's failure to consider what will truly benefit the children involved. The father should be mature enough to settle matters within the household ("He's apologised and we've accepted, so there's an end to it") and leave any emotional outbursts to the mother.

I remember one time I gave my son a fearsome telling-off when he was about three years old. It was the only time I ever got that angry with him; once was enough, it seems. Strict discipline by a dad enables children to draw a clear line between what is acceptable and what is not. It teaches them the boundaries that they must not overstep for fear of causing trouble for others and getting into trouble themselves.

In that sense, fathers must accept that they are society's first line of defence against misbehaviour. When a father scolds his children and tells them that they must never repeat the offensive behaviour, children tend to observe those limits. I am convinced that it is a father's job to lay down those lines, and that is why a father must not be his children's buddy.

In this chapter, I have written about the "role of the father," but this must be interpreted creatively in families without a father. In these cases, the mother must be the father figure. Single mothers and divorcees may ask the children's grandparents who live nearby to take on the sterner, fatherly role. In conclusion, children need someone in their lives who is a severe father figure, regardless of who actually plays that role.

024: Why Are We Shy in the Face of Praise?

Children love to be praised, and praise develops enthusiasm. Therefore, I recommend that you praise your children for anything and everything they do right, even something as minor as eating their vegetables. "Well done, don't they taste good? And you ate them all!"

I also think that it's a good idea to praise your children soon after a reprimand. Have them perform some task, even if it is simply to give you an excuse to praise them, and say something like, "Atta boy." This will ease the sting of discipline and they will sleep well that night. Let your children experience praise and affirmation in all kinds of situations.

Strangely however, Japanese people are terrible at praising: We don't know how to praise others and we don't know how to handle praise when it is directed at us. It is a distinctive defect in the Japanese psyche.

We have a native speaker of English who teaches at our kindergarten, and one day I asked him how to praise others in English. He told me the most popular phrase was "well done," followed by "excellent job." He also mentioned "good work," which is similar to the "good job" we often use in Japan, but I was surprised to find out that "good job" is not always used in a positive sense overseas. Finally, there was "fantastic," which I assume is used when the person giving praise is particularly excited.

My impression of these phrases is that, with the exception of "fantastic," they all focus on outcomes of some action. Personally, I like "fantastic," but apparently this is only used sparingly.

One phrase really surprised me: "I am proud of you." These words do not come easily to the Japanese tongue, no matter how often we may hear the expression in foreign movies.

In any case, the range of Japanese praise phrases is limited and we often struggle to express our affirmation of others.

Having said that, however, seeing children makes me want to praise them to bits. Even something as simple as sitting quietly and listening to the teacher makes me want to pat them on the head and say, "What a tremendous display of listening!" Unlike straight-laced adults, children cannot hide their pleasure at being praised even for trivial things.

I cannot remember my parents ever praising me when I was young. Maybe that is why I still don't know how to react when somebody praises me today. For instance, when playing golf (my favourite pastime), I am quick to say, "Good shot!" when somebody hits the ball well, but I am uncomfortable when someone says the same to me. I guess this is because I am secretly convinced that my good shot will inevitably be followed by a stream of terrible ones. But even with my discomfort in the face of praise, I cannot remain motivated without finding something that I can praise myself for and I need the occasional words of encouragement like, "Good shot."

The same goes for children: Praise and affirmation from others helps them develop internal criteria to judge whether they are personally satisfied with what they are doing. So, please praise your children. It can be done directly or indirectly (i.e. "Such-and-such said you did really well today"). In fact, report third-party praise to your child and I guarantee that you will get a happy face in return. I believe that children who receive lots of praise in their early years grow up with a strong sense of self-affirmation, which, as an adult, translates into boldness and positivity. So, praise everything and anything you can think of because it will make your children more positive while deepening the bond you share with them.

025: A Message to Those With Special Needs Children

In recent years, it has become increasingly common in kindergarten to en-rol children diagnosed with developmental disorders into regular schools. This is known as mainstreaming. I have no reservations about working with people who have disabilities; in fact, I run a facility for people with disabilities in addition to the kindergarten.

Nonetheless, I am well aware that mainstreaming is extremely difficult and poses a challenge to the education community. For instance, in one case, we hired a teacher for the special needs children, but ended up hav-ing to provide her with psychological care. In the end, she resigned and managed to forge another career, but it just goes to show that under the current system, there are high hurdles to hiring teachers to care for special needs children.

Of course, there have been successful cases as well, and that is something I am eager for parents who are worried about their disabled child's educa-tion to know.

The following is a letter I received from the mother of a boy who came to us when he was three years old. It is reprinted with her permission.

> From the time he was born, Taro [name changed] cried a lot and he wouldn't sleep well at night. People told me this was typical of many babies so for the first few years, I didn't really worry about it. Then, when Taro was three years old and I was pregnant with our second child, those concerns that I had pushed aside came flooding back and I decided to seek advice about Taro's education from the city government. As a result, we decided to put Taro in an early childhood intervention facility.

> Later on, when I was wondering whether we should send Taro to kindergarten, one of the neighbourhood mothers, whose child attended Makoto Kindergarten,

told me about the diverse curriculum there, which included things like violin lessons. According to those mothers, their children enjoyed a positive experience at Makoto Kindergarten. It sounded like something that Taro would be interested in and a kindergarten he could enjoy, so I knocked on their door half expecting they would refuse to enrol a child with Taro's challenges.

Contrary to my fears, the principal and the teachers listened and advised me with great sincerity, ultimately recommending that I enrol Taro, so I did.

Everything was going well until the summer vacation when I got to spend more time with Taro. I noticed that there had been no change in the behaviours that had concerned me before he began kindergarten, so I made the difficult decision to have him examined at a hospital.

Taro was diagnosed with pervasive developmental disorder, a condition on the autism spectrum characterised by delayed language development, communication difficulties, and sudden, repetitive movements.

Although we had suspected something was wrong, it still came as a terrible shock to receive this news. I suppose we had hoped that if we ignored the reality we could somehow get by, but the news disabused us of that notion and now we were confronted with the question: What on earth are we going to do?

At the same time, we were strongly aware that we were the only ones who could protect Taro and that there was no time for moping; we had to do everything we could for our son.

We were told that it would be best for Taro to finish out his first year of kindergarten at Makoto and transfer to a special needs kindergarten starting with the new school year in April. The final decision, however, was ours to make. It was a very, very difficult decision to make, not least because Taro loved kindergarten and was so happy when he got on the bus every morning. At sports days and recitals, Taro managed to play his part with the help of his peers and this had helped build up his confidence.

However, we thought that a specialist institution would provide better developmental treatment in light of his diagnosed condition and decided that Taro would transfer schools the following April. When I visited principal Yamamura, told him of our decision, and thanked him for all he had done, he was most gracious, telling us that he would not say goodbye. "This is not the end," he said, "and Taro is welcome back at any time." We were tremendously encouraged by his kind words.

So, Taro began attending his new kindergarten in April and was placed in the second year of kindergarten (kindergartens in Japan are either two or three year programs). There were many other children with autism at the new school, some of whom had more serious conditions than Taro. I suppose every parent thinks that their child is better than everyone else, but it seemed to me that the new kindergarten would not be stimulating enough for Taro. But it was Taro himself who appeared most underwhelmed. After only a month, he began to refuse to get out of the car when we dropped him off in the morning.

We insisted that Taro keep going, though, telling him that this would be the best and most enjoyable place for him once he got used to it. But, far from settling down, he became more distracted than ever before and was nothing like the happy boy who had attended Makoto Kindergarten.

It was then that we realised that we had made the wrong choice. We went back to principal Yamamura and asked to re-enrol Taro. He welcomed us as warmly as the first time we met, saying, "We were hoping you would come back."

I am sure that Taro has been a real handful for the good people at Makoto Kindergarten.

He struggles with group interaction and finds it impossible to sit still on his own. Somehow, though, he has made friends in kindergarten and turned that setting into his daily reality. Kindergarten is, without a doubt, an integral part of his identity now.

Taro's growth in confidence came thanks to the lovely teachers who would help him out whenever anything happened and his friends who provided such a wonderful example for him. Initially, enrolling Taro in kindergarten was more for our own satisfaction than something that he wanted, and at times, I feared that we had set the bar too high for him, and ended up inconveniencing others to boot. But there is no doubt that the stimulations of kindergarten sparked a gradual change in Taro. To my mind, the proof of that progress came in his graduation speech: "I want to become a chef and open a cake shop," he said in his own, unprompted words.

I know that Taro's presence in kindergarten inconvenienced his teachers and classmates, and I am grateful for the way they treated him. In particular, the understanding shown by the teachers and their sensitive explanations for the other children about Taro's condition were instrumental in ensuring that his classmates treated him with kindness.

In a surprising reversal of roles, the other mothers thanked me on graduation day, saying that Taro's presence had made their children kind and gentle. I was grateful for their generosity.

Children with disabilities all face unique challenges, and it is thanks to the teachers who tailored their care to meet Taro's individual needs that he was able to attend kindergarten right through to graduation. Attending and completing kindergarten was a step forward in Taro's life, and an achievement that our family will cherish. We can never thank you enough for all you have done for us over Taro's three years in kindergarten.

Notwithstanding those kind words, it is Taro's parents and not Makoto Kindergarten who deserve praise for their strength and resolve in the face of Taro's challenges. Their unflinching acceptance of Taro's developmental disorder and their openly pragmatic search for ways to help their boy and find the best solutions for him is what helped to make this outcome a positive one. Indeed, Taro's case has given all of us at our kindergarten confidence in our teaching and support activities.

026: Sometimes You Have to Do Things You Don't Want To

Here is a poem for parents who are worried about letting go of your children as they enter kindergarten, school, or the workforce.

Rain, by Yasujiro Nomura

> Rain
> Must fall
> Even on poop.
> It has to,
> Even if it doesn't want to.
> Nobody else
> Will do it instead.

> (Source: Chichi Magazine, October 2008, Chichi Publishing)

It's only seven lines long but it expresses a universal truth in the phrase, "It has to, even if it doesn't want to." This poem is an observation of how life is not all fun and games but includes hardship and sorrow as well.

You could even say that hardship and sorrow are what makes the good times good. Parents must be ready to deal with the tough times as well as the good times. Instead of bemoaning times of hardship and strife, parents should stop focusing on their misfortune and take on a new perspective; things happen for a reason and parents should identify the lessons they and their children can learn from those difficult situations.

In fact, I think the quality most lacking in today's parents is the courage to change their perspective when faced by adverse circumstances. They seem unwilling to take full responsibility for their children's actions, and that is why we see people trying to blame others or say, "My child would never do that."

When your children encounter adversity, it is up to you, the parents, to help them find a solution. Yes, you may have to resign yourself to disappointment or worse. Regardless of which your child may be, sometimes the parents of the instigator and the victim have to come together and clear the air for their children. Just like the rain, you have to do it even if you don't want to.

Your children will one day have to leave the warm embrace of home and face the harsh realities of the world, where they must survive away from your helping hands. You will not be there to do everything for them.

This is most apparent in April, the traditional start of the new work and school year, when parents are often heard remarking that, although it is a time of great excitement, it is also a time when we must steel ourselves against upcoming responsibilities. The time when our children enter kindergarten, school, or the workforce is the time when we must let go, they say; we cannot keep them under constant watch anymore and we must be ready to leave them in society's hands.

Try re-reading the poem at the beginning of this chapter, but this time replace "rain" with "children" and "poop" with "hardship and sorrow." Nobody's parents can do everything for them once they take their first steps out into society; you've got to let them go.

027: Your Child Will Become a Total Stranger During Adolescence

It is hard to define the exact beginning and end of adolescence; suffice it to say that it is a time when children place more value on their peer relationships than their family. There is no need for you to reject the decisions made by your adolescent children or how their friends influence their behaviour. Having said that, however, you should make them understand that their actions (even those taken under the influence of friends) have consequences. In other words, it is important to develop their awareness that they are responsible for the actions that they choose to take.

Dialogue with your children becomes difficult during adolescence. Parents must also be careful of how they speak and act: Never say anything to your children that you would not want people to say to you. Use your common sense and lead by example in not saying things that society considers to be unacceptable.

However difficult it may be, talking to your children is the only way you are going to keep up with what is going on in their lives and minds. Indeed, this is a phase that will task your imagination like never before. Parents must try to decipher everything about their children from the few mumbled words they get out of their teenagers.

Conversations between parents and children drop off during puberty. This is a concern for parents because it is a time when children's minds are rife with worries and problems. Parents need to be on the lookout for telltale signs that their teenager is struggling with weighty issues and is searching for solutions.

Although this is a time when parent-child relations are prone to become strained, tell your teenagers that they can come to you for advice at any time if things get tough. Other than that, be ready to accept the fact that there may be no communication at all between the two of you for a long time.

One of the most important things in dealing with adolescents is that you can prepare in advance for the difficulties and crises of puberty. Showering your children with love from an early age and teaching them the difference between right and wrong in those first few years provides the foundation which enables them to overcome their teenage problems on their own. You can't go back and do it once your children have already reached adolescence. Looking ahead and learning with your children during their toddler and childhood years will require imagination about the challenges that they will face in their teen years.

028: Why We Encourage Arguments Between Kids in Kindergarten

It's a funny thing to say, but I welcome those instances when kids in my kindergarten get into fights or get involved in bullying. What I mean is that it's better that these things happen in kindergarten than later on, such as when the children are in the latter stages of elementary school.

I say it is good because it presents a learning opportunity. When these incidents arise, we are forced to consider the underlying meanings and how we should deal with these matters in the future. There are chances for everyone, parents included, to gain experience in resolving problems, clear the area of animosity, and move things in a positive direction.

My basic approach to resolving childhood issues is to encourage everyone to think about the future. Dwelling on the past does not make for good
child raising; we need to concentrate on tomorrow.

The same applies to children who refuse to go to school: If this problem
arises, it is better that it happens earlier than later. In these cases, the earlier
you discover that your child has a tendency to say things like "I refuse to
go to school," the better. These are signs of a deeper issue, and when he or
she starts talking about not going to school again in the future, you will
recognise it as a sign of something else.

Early recognition enables early resolution. For instance, if your child
throws a tantrum and refuses to go to kindergarten, try something different. Why not say, "Okay, you can go tomorrow and I'll get your teacher to
come and pick you up," or "I'll drop you off and take you home via a different, special route?" Similarly, bullying in this age group tends to stop as
soon as you have a word with the perpetrator. Children, particularly young
children, react positively to adult efforts to find solutions to their problems.

But as children enter elementary and middle school, this is no longer
the case. By this stage, children have already developed their sense of self
and have a budding desire to rebel against adult values. It is very hard to
overturn these feelings once they have set in, and adolescence only compli-
cates things. Increasingly complex environments are making solutions more
difficult. That is why when a worried mother of one of our children says,
"Little Taro is refusing to go to kindergarten," I say, "Oh, good!" If you
can identify your children's tendencies and issues and set them on the right
path while they are still in kindergarten, I think that they will turn out all
right because the experience of having overcome difficulties will help them
develop greater confidence.

029: The Sound of the Wind Can't Be Taught

Listening develops a child's imagination and ability to think. As children
get older, they begin to paint mental images of what they've heard and this
encourages them to question things that don't seem quite right. I think this
may be one of the most advanced of human abilities.

We already know that reading stories aloud to your newborn baby stimulates the areas of his or her brain dedicated to language. Listening develops
the brain, and reading to your child is an effective way of doing so.

In that sense, I think that it is important for children to listen to a range
of things and not just to converse with family members, but also to listen to
the sounds of nature, such as the sound of the rain, the sound of the wind,
the sound of rustling leaves, the sound of trees dancing in the wind, the
sound of birdsong, etc. Hearing all of these sounds encourages children to
imagine, and they will serve as the triggers that, in later years, will remind
them of their childhood.

It's a great idea to talk with your child as you listen to the sounds of
nature together, using phrases such as "I think the thunder has gone off in
that direction," "Oh, here comes a big thunderclap," "I think it's going to
rain," etc. Listening to different sounds together with your child lets you
engage in a dialogue as equals. In that sense, the sounds of the natural
environment are like music: You can both share in the enjoyment of the
same sounds. I believe that the shared experience of listening and watching together provides children with a source of inner strength to support
them through life.

There is a limit to the experiences we can provide in kindergarten. For
instance, to listen to the wind you have to go outside when it is windy, but,
with only 800 hours to work with each year (four hours a day, 200 days
a year) and so much to get through, there just isn't enough time for us to
spend listening to the wind at school. Therefore, I encourage parents to
engage in these activities at home.

We live in an age of information overload. The rise of the internet and
the widespread availability of mobile phones has brought the world much
closer, and today's children will grow up in a society that runs on information. But there are many pitfalls of having too much information, and we
are prone to thinking that when we have seen one we have seen them all.
That is why, now more than ever, we need to open our ears to the sounds
of the natural environment.

Incidentally, let me recommend another way in which you can enjoy
the sounds of the world around us. *Ikiru*, by Shuntaro Tanikawa, is of my
favourite poems; I love the way that his very words evoke a range of sounds.
I highly recommend it.

030: Parents Are Responsible for How They Have Taught Their Children

I sometimes wonder how I would react if one of my children was assaulted or was arrested for assaulting somebody else.

What would you do? Try to imagine how you would feel.

I find myself incapable of imagining how I would react if one of my children were arrested for assault. I can, however, predict my reaction if my child was the victim of an assault: I assume I would get together with the parents of all the children involved in the incident and we would talk it through, focusing on the events that led up to the assault and what it would mean to us as parents.

The assault on your child may well be the result of something that you taught them to do. For instance, it may be that your child took the beating because you instilled a message into him or her that he or she must never react with violence, even in the face of violence. In a case like this, you should praise your child for doing as he or she was taught and not hitting back despite extenuating circumstances.

My point is that parents must take full responsibility for the lessons they teach their children. Taking responsibility means praising your child for behaving as he or she was taught. We must always commend our children when they do as they have been told.

Some parents may worry that their children are left unable to defend themselves because of how they were taught. If this is a concern, then tell your children that they should do whatever is necessary to protect themselves if they are in physical or mental danger, and promise that you will take responsibility for their actions if the need arises.

In the end, it comes down to how far you are willing to analyse the processes leading up to incidents like this. If an incident occurred as a result of the way that you discipline your child, your first task is to take responsibility. You can discuss how to resolve the situation later, whether it involves teaching your child how to make up with the other child or maintaining his or her distance for a while until emotions cool down.

031: Why Parents Should Observe the Rings of Saturn

I used to hate science, but have come to take an interest in it in later life. My interest began after I became a father and I realised how ignorant I was when I tried to explain nature and the world around us to my children. I realised I needed to study and, as I did, it piqued my interest in the natural sciences.

Many readers may know the story called *The Big Dipper*. In it, a young girl gives her grandfather a ladleful of water during a severe drought. The ladle suddenly sparkles with seven beautiful diamonds and flies up into the sky where it becomes seven twinkling stars in the shape of a ladle, the Big Dipper.

You can help consolidate your children's budding knowledge by reading them a picture book like *The Big Dipper* and then going outside at night to look at the skies, pointing out the Big Dipper constellation and telling them that these are the stars they heard about in the book. However, parents must first learn and experience these things themselves if they hope to teach their children.

In kindergarten, we often have stargazing sessions. Seeing Saturn and the stripy surface of Jupiter for the first time through a telescope is an awe-inspiring experience for both parents and children. I tell parents that for the children it is enough to simply enjoy the view through the telescope, but the parents must observe more carefully. If they are genuinely moved by what they have seen, then they should tell their children how beautiful they thought it was.

Unfortunately, at times like these, many grown-ups try to force a lesson, demanding answers from their children. "Did you see something? What was it like?" This is a bad habit; the important thing is whether you, the parents, saw something, and not your children.

I call it a bad habit because it is vital that parents experience these things for themselves before trying to teach their children. Learn to express yourself in words that your children will understand. You can help consolidate your child's experience into knowledge through your own enthusiasm for the surprises and wonders of nature.

032: Why Some People Smell Their Food Before They Eat

Have you ever noticed that some people always smell their food before they eat it? The human sense of smell is a vital part of the way we eat; smelling our food not only tells us if it is likely to be tasty, but it is also part of our instinct to determine whether or not it is safe. If this sense weakens, we end up eating things without knowing whether they are good for us.

I believe that modern humans, children included, are losing their sense of smell. I suspect one reason is that more and more people have never eaten freshly harvested food. The more we experience real fresh food, the more sensitive we become to food that has gone off. That is why I try to organise farm trips for the children in kindergarten and try to allow them to experience eating freshly harvested vegetables whenever possible.

Once, I was walking in the forest with my children, when we came upon a wild chocolate vine. "Do you want to try the fruit?" I asked, and offered one to them. The fruit of the chocolate vine is purple on the outside and white and fleshy on the inside. "Don't forget to spit out the seeds," I reminded them and watched carefully to see how they would react to this new and strange fruit.

"It's yummy!" they cried, taking great pleasure in spitting out a stream of seeds. At that time, it occurred to me that these experiences are very important to a child's development. There are some things they should discover for themselves rather than being spoon-fed.

I once heard about a farmer who grew some of the most delicious apples in Aomori, Japan's famed apple orchard region. Apparently, the first thing he did before planting the trees was to eat the soil in various locations. By eating the soil, he was able to imagine which of the locations would produce the tastiest apples. Perhaps that man has a sixth sense for these things, but in any case, it is an interesting example of how people possess the ability to imagine things.

To fully develop our senses, we really need to go outside and watch, listen, touch, taste, and smell the natural environment. At home, we can augment this by providing our children with freshly harvested seasonal food and encouraging them to smell and taste the different ingredients, a culinary education of sorts. For instance, when cooking a meal, why not show your children the individual ingredients? I believe incorporating these little exchanges between parents and children into one's daily life will surely come back to them as they grow up and have children of their own.

033: A Story That Needs No Discussion

Kenji Miyazawa's *Night of the Milky Way Railway* is a famous children's tale and has been adapted into a popular picture book.

I wasn't sure what the story was trying to say when I first read the book, but my daughter loved it and would ask me to read it again and again. I thought that was curious because it is a very sad story, but I suppose there was something about it that tugged at her heart.

Although you may be familiar with this story, I guess the ultimate message of *Night of the Milky Way Railway* is that real value lies in human kindness, serving society, and helping others.

Personally, the message from *Night of the Milky Way Railway* that resonated most with me was the importance of having a strong will. For instance, we often hear about how the secret behind the successful farmer's ability to grow tasty fruit is not his innovative cultivation techniques, but his utter determination to make quality produce. Also, we often hear how a steam train runs not on burning coal, but on the dedication of the people behind it. These sayings illustrate the importance of will and determination.

They say that actions speak loudest of all, but all actions begin with the will to do or achieve something. As such, I assume that a positive will leads to positive action and that a negative will lead to negative action.

Night of the Milky Way Railway is a sad tale that ends with the death of the character Campanella; however, the story also reminds us of the importance of thinking and aspiring to do the right thing. It is a story that needs no added discussion or opinion. When I read it to my daughter, I did not feel the need to ask her what she thought of it; I just let her enjoy it in her own way. It is the kind of story that reveals its qualities with every read.

034: The Common Misconception Regarding Children's "Limitless Potential"

We often hear that children have limitless potential, but that is an exaggeration. After all, life itself is finite and nothing is limitless, so let's just say that children have great potential.

Saying children have limitless potential may sound very nice, but it is also the reason that parents give for burdening their children with overblown expectations. Let's not get carried away.

In kindergarten, we used to have a girl whose parents wanted her to become an actress and had signed her up with a production company. The father would go berserk at the slightest injury in kindergarten. They believed in their child's limitless potential and dreamed that she would become an actress, and this had made them excessively sensitive to the idea that she might pick up a disfiguring scratch or a scar in kindergarten.

I doubt this parental attitude would benefit a young child. At that age, surely there are other things they need to be learning.

Obviously, we in the education sector seek to fully develop each child's potential, but we are wary of the "limitless potential" concept since it is prone to be interpreted as "let the children run riot." Early childhood is the time when children must learn boundaries which include the customs and rules we follow as a society. They need to learn these norms, making me loath to use terms like "limitless potential."

The same goes for the expression "individuality." Respect for individuals and developing each child's individuality is all well and good, but it does not lend itself to the group dynamic that children must learn to survive schools and kindergartens. We do encourage the development of unique abilities, but I do not think that this is the same thing as individuality. In my opinion, individuality can only be developed after children have mastered the basics. They must first be showered with love from their parents and have learned to behave in public without disturbing the collective harmony of their surroundings.

Perhaps your child shows some potential on the violin and you want him or her to take lessons to develop that potential. That is fine, but I would prefer you to take those lessons elsewhere. School and kindergarten are primarily for learning the manners and rules of social interaction. Here, our goal is to develop a child's ability to listen to others and speak his or her own opinions appropriately. They are where children learn the correct balance between consideration for others and self-empowerment, a skill they will need to become upstanding citizens in later life.

035: Walking Their Way Through Life

It appears to me that today's parents are too quick to pick up their children when they don't feel like walking. Once a child learns to walk, he or she should do so as much as possible.

The world is not all paved and smooth; there are mountain trails, grass tracks, and bumpy footpaths as well as asphalt roads, and children benefit the most by walking on all of these and learning to feel the differences.

Parents do their children a disservice by "protecting" them from the dangers of bumpy surfaces, and I think that making them walk on their own two feet sets them on the path to independence. After all, children want to use their newfound abilities, whether it be talking or walking, so I recommend that parents (especially the younger ones) put their kids down and let them walk since doing every little thing to cater to their children will ultimately spoil them.

Make your child walk and, if they trip up, the pain of a skinned knee will be a lesson in being brave when things happen. Of course, once they have successfully walked to their destination, you can sweep them up and hug them plenty. It is important that children learn lessons through exposure to the challenges and rewards of life at a young age.

You may wonder what has piqued me enough to say such a thing. Well, I get the feeling that more and more of our kindergarten and nursery school children are unable to walk properly on the up-and-down trails when we go on nearby nature walks. Obviously that does not apply to everyone as many children handle the uneven surfaces just fine, but sometimes I am amazed to see children who are unable to keep their footing or who are unable to adjust their pace.

Children develop a little every day at their own speeds. Sometimes they cry and complain when things don't turn out the way they would like, but that is just part of growing up, rather than something to prevent growth. There is a difference between kindness and interfering in your child's development, and I urge all parents to consider which side of that line their actions fall on.

036: Is Physical Punishment Absolutely Wrong?

These days, the issue of physical punishment has been placed firmly in the general conscience. Physical punishment is being roundly castigated as a terrible thing, but I am wary of this movement. Needless to say, excessive physical punishment crosses the line to plain violence and cannot be excused, but I have serious doubts about the view that all physical punishment should be banned. Physical punishment is not needed in kindergarten, but completely eliminating it from elementary, middle, and high schools makes the teacher's job very difficult. Readers will surely understand that not every child behaves just because the teacher tells them to, and one unruly child in class can often cause others to misbehave.

Come to think of it, we do not hear about this "problem" with corporal punishment outside of Japan. In the United States, for instance, they do not share Japan's issue with first graders where new entrants to elementary school are unable to sit quietly and do as the teacher tells them to during class. This is not because America has no unruly children; rather, it is because they have a system to deal with children who cause trouble for the class. In Japan, we do not have this system. Therefore, if troublesome children were removed from the classroom, it would not deal with the root cause but simply dump the problem onto the shoulders of their parents.

Getting rid of physical punishment instead of the troublesome children themselves would soon result in Japanese schools devolving into chaos. If schools were forced to teach problem children alongside their more disciplined peers and were banned from using physical punishment as a deterrent, how would teachers keep control of their classes? Teachers are human, too, and although they are required to be role models for their students, that requirement must be based on the expectation that the students themselves have first acquired the basic manners and attitudes needed to participate in a social environment. The shrill calls of opposition to physical punishment that we hear from populist television experts do nothing to contribute to a viable solution. Surely, this has been illustrated by the never-ending stream of tragic incidents.

In fact, why should the debate regarding physical punishment take place in society at large? I believe that it makes more sense to establish a system to provide children with more opportunities to experience various aspects of society and to learn the manners, language, and behaviour required when dealing with others. For an example of this, we need only to look as far as Europe. Austria has a system of civil service called Zivildienst, under which youths gain experience through obligatory community service in a group such as the Red Cross for a year. Zivildienst is an alternative to military service, and youths may opt to do a six-month stint of military service instead of community service.

How should we view physical punishment? I believe that it is an issue for each individual family to consider. We are not able to raise our children all alone; in my case, my local community played a major role in helping my children develop, and I am grateful. Therefore, if a child is out of line, I believe that he or she needs to learn what is acceptable within social relationships, even if a slap on the cheek is what it takes to instil that lesson.

037: Japan's Future is Created in Kindergartens

Recently, I often hear how junior high school students have lost interest in science-related subjects. My guess is that this is caused by a lack of exposure (in class or through experiments) to nature which should have nurtured a child's natural curiosity in the sciences.

In London, I once met a Japanese businessman outside my hotel. He told me that the electronic displays used in museums worldwide, including the British Museum, were now manufactured in South Korea. Very few, he said, were still made in Japan.

He told me that Japan had experienced a large-scale brain drain a while ago, in which many people who had retired or were laid off from Japanese companies were headhunted by South Korean businesses. Ten or 15 years later, South Korean products became very prominent in world markets. This gentleman was clearly worried about Japan's future and urged me to use my position as a kindergarten principal to better educate Japan's future generations. I returned to Japan very concerned about this move away from the sciences and the general drop in Japan's academic ability, wondering how Japan would compete in the global arena.

Japan was once a manufacturing powerhouse and technology was a central pillar of its national strategy. I worry about how we will regain our former prowess. It is a serious problem, and from an educator's standpoint,

I believe that we must begin by laying the foundations on which children can develop their intellectual curiosity and ambition. In that sense, both homes and school are ideal places for children to develop the fundamental strengths that will enable them to subsequently develop their abilities as they mature. Without curiosity and ambition, children cannot hope to succeed once they enter the workforce. Nowadays, we are finally seeing an increase in events that show children how to have fun with science and experiments, but I think that schools and kindergartens need to provide more of such opportunities at an even younger age.

Parents, in the meanwhile, should observe and talk about nature with their children, even if it is simply talking about the weather or catching insects together. Natural, everyday conversation is a fine way to teach kids about nature and the environment ("Gee, it got a little cooler once we entered the forest, didn't it?"), and serves to trigger further interest in natural sciences. And if you can help your children ponder and resolve the scientific questions which arise in your daily life, well, who could ask for more?

038: The Importance of Basic Phrases

I constantly encourage parents to teach their children a few all-important "basic phrases" while they are still young. These are phrases like "please," "thank you," and "I'm sorry;" they take only a moment to say, yet are expressions to smooth and soothe the paths of daily life. They are easy words and are not too much to expect children as young as three and four years old to use effectively.

Children should learn basic manners at home, including greetings, answering when spoken to, and keeping their things tidy. The good thing about these actions is that they should be second nature, yet do not require too much thought. They are, however, fundamental requirements so it is important that parents and children observe these little rituals.

It is not realistic to expect kindergartens and nursery schools to instil these basic values without help from the children's families. The teaching of these fundamentals that pave the way for later life must begin at home, and kindergartens, nursery schools, and grade schools can play a reinforcing role.

Let me give you an example to illustrate this point. In kindergarten, we have overnight camps where we pitch tents and sleep outside. Activities include catching fish (by hand) from a pool, skewering them, and cooking them for dinner. One time, one of the children said, "Eww, gross!" I told her that, although catching a live fish might not be the most pleasant experience, she was wrong to disrespect the animal.

"You're going to eat the fish, so you could at least say 'itadakimasu' as a sign of thanks to the fish for giving its life to sustain yours." I honestly don't know whether the children understood the significance of saying "itadakimasu," but I believe we grown-ups should explain these things to kids anyway.

Phrases like "thank you," "I'm sorry," and "itadakimasu" show our appreciation and consideration of others. Making children recite these words makes them aware that we share the world with others, both people and animals, and that we support each other through life. Teaching children these "basic phrases" is one of a parent's most important roles because it instils the fundamental manners that your children will need to survive in the future.

039: Automation and the Decline of Self-affirming Experiences

We live in an age of uber-convenience where even tasks as mundane as running the bath can be done automatically with the push of a button. I grew up in a poor household where we had to heat the bath by lighting a fire underneath the tub; one of my chores was to collect the firewood. I hated this task, but now I see it as a role in the family which allowed me to fit in as one of the clan. Fulfilling my task benefited everyone, and that gave me great satisfaction. In a way, because we were poor, a happy side effect was that everyone in our family had to pitch in and that everyone had their role.

Naturally, I also had to help out in the fields. My job was to fill big cans with the manure we used as fertiliser and carry them to our field on a pole across my shoulders. There would always be some spillage, but I steeled myself for the 20-minute walk. My father never rewarded me for this labour, but I remember being very happy when neighbourhood "uncles" and "aunties" would give me a mandarin or another snack along with a kind word of encouragement.

I'm not discussing the merits or demerits of compensating children for their chores, but want to emphasise the importance of recognising their effort. Not only does affirmation motivate children, but it also helps to link a child's sense of satisfaction at completing an assigned chore with his or her sense of being a part of the family.

The young mothers and fathers of today were raised by parents who lived through Japan's "economic miracle." They spoiled their children because they wanted their kids to have something better than the drudgery that they had experienced. Perhaps that is why so many of today's parents lack confidence in their parenting skills. You should give your child chores around the house. When your children ask for something, do not just give it to them. Have them take on tasks that will benefit the whole family. For instance, they could fetch the newspaper every morning or clear the table before meals, anything that they would be capable of doing. Then, perhaps after a week, reward them with praise for their work and buy them something. This is an effective way to enable your child to experience small steps of success.

It is just as important that parents also feel a sense of self-affirmation. To that end, make it a point to be punctual. Do not blame your child for your tardiness. Don't' make excuses like, "I couldn't be on time because my child is so young." Since you now have a child, plan ahead and take into account that you'll need extra time. Change your lifestyle. You are now a parent with responsibilities, so your habits should reflect that.

040: Imagining the Unimaginable to Avoid Tragedy

As always, the news is never short of stories on bullying and suicide.

I am sure that many parents share my pain upon hearing the many stories of child suicide in the news. However, I doubt that many parents seriously think that this issue might concern them. Parents should seriously consider the possibility that this could indeed be about their child. Then, they would finally start to appreciate the unfathomable grief of such a terrible outcome and begin to consider what they could do in order to avoid such a tragedy. In my opinion, that is the starting point in reducing child suicides.

The prevention of suicide is a matter of risk management in that it is imperative to think and act before something happens. Risk management involves imagining the worst-case scenarios; in this case, asking the question, "What if my child committed suicide?" Only by imagining the unimaginable can you take the action needed to prevent this. Parents who miss seeing the subtle signs of danger are ignoring the risks and blithely believing that their child would never do such a thing.

Children go through times of crisis, typically in the fourth year of elementary school, the second year of junior high school, or approximately six months after entering junior high school. Parents should pay particular attention to their children at these stages to ensure that their children are adjusting well to their circumstances, and should anything appear to be wrong, they should not ignore it. Careful attention and action in these situations can go a long way towards preventing tragic outcomes like suicide.

Nobody will tell you if your child is experiencing a crisis; you will need to keep an eye on them and determine in advance the specific things that you, as a parent, should do in the worst-case scenario.

I would also like to talk about extracurricular activities at schools since many children have killed themselves over bullying and hazing in such clubs.

I believe extracurricular activities come under pressure from three sources. First, there is the school; second, there is the teacher who coaches or is otherwise in charge of the club. These are both a factor because for instance, winning a big tournament would bring honour to the school and the teacher in charge. The third source of pressure is parents. After all, every parent would prefer that their child was a regular on the starting team rather than a bench warmer.

These third-party egos can sometimes pile on the pressure, leading to tragic consequences. A child buffeted by pressure from three directions will quickly find that he or she has nowhere to escape to, and the danger arises that he or she may contemplate suicide as a way out. It is up to the parents to notice when something is wrong and to act before things go too far. If, for example, your child is dropped from the starting line-up or stripped of the captaincy, you need to relieve the pressure, rather than increase it. This may mean taking drastic action that could even affect your child's chances of going to the high school or university of his or her choice, such as making him or her quit the team.

The lurid stories of tragic suicides that we read about in the media often lay the blame exclusively on the teacher in charge of the deceased student's extracurricular club, but I have my doubts about this. Ultimately, it is up to the parents to protect their children, and I urge you to make tough decisions regardless of what teachers and children may say to challenge you.

041: Teaching Three-Year-Olds the Value of Work

One phenomenon that I believe poses a major problem for our society's future is the way that the increasing number of unemployed youths is being explained as an incompatibility between job seekers and jobs. There are any number of vacancies on offer at Hello Work job centres nationwide, but people come up with all sorts of excuses for rejecting these positions, including that they are not interested, the compensation package is not good enough, there are not enough holidays, and it involves getting dirty.

The facility for people with special needs that I run in addition to the kindergarten struggled for a time to find new caregivers to work there. In particular, we were unable to attract young people. It made me want to shout, "You don't know what a job will be like until you try it! Don't reject a job without giving it a try!"

Young people today pick and choose based on their own narrow experiences and knowledge without even trying things out. Even if they do try things, they are likely to quit after three days. How do they know things would not have been different in a year if they had given the job a chance? Patience is a virtue, as the saying goes, and I think that we need to teach children the benefits of perseverance.

We have set patterns of behaviour for those in the special needs facility, just like the daily routines in kindergarten. We wake up our residents, help them eat, bathe, and assist them in the toilet, then help them later with their next meal, and so on and so forth. It is repetitive work but the joy of making a difference in people's lives enables us to persevere and find positive rewards in our jobs.

Of course, all jobs, not just caregiving, exist because they are in some way necessary for society. Our jobs are not a right; we work at what we do because society lets us. We need to instil appreciation for the privilege of working in today's youths.

To that end, I encourage parents to tell their children about how mum and dad contribute to society through their work. Show them how every single job is significant in some way, and I believe that they will be less likely to shy away from work when they grow up.

042: The Importance of Setting Boundaries

Children are often told to neatly line up their shoes after taking them off when they come inside. We are always reminding children of this in kindergarten, but it really is something that should be taught at home. Some families believe that it is more thoughtful to position a guest's shoes so that they will be easy to put on again, so we try not to be too strict about how the shoes are lined up and just focus on ensuring that they are neat. The same goes for toy building blocks. Teach the children that neatness has benefits by showing them that they can't build a tall tower if the blocks are not lined up neatly. It is a lesson relevant throughout life. The same holds for why factories are so fussy about order and tidiness; the quicker a worker can find and access his or her tools, the safer and more efficient work becomes.

We teach boundaries and the beauty of keeping things neat and tidy for a reason. I urge parents to instil this lesson as part of one's daily life so as to nurture an internal desire to keep things clean and neat and to teach children to feel good when everything is in order.

Once upon a time (but less so today), we were taught not to step on the edges of tatami floor mats. This custom began with the warrior and merchant families of the old generations, whose tatami mats were bound with decorative edging that bore the family crest. To step on that was to step on the faces of your ancestors. Now, tatami mats are edged with a range of patterns, such as flowers, plants, and even animal patterns, but the point of the custom remains the same: For example, to teach children to tread softly and with consideration for flowers, plants, and animals. In other words, teaching children not to step on the edge of tatami mats was a way of instilling kindness towards others.

Of course, there will always be people who find boundaries constricting, but I am convinced that children who are taught to be clean, polite, and punctual from an early age will grow up to be capable workers in later life.

My work brings me into contact with a broad range of people, and there are times when I look at someone and wonder, sometimes in admiration and sometimes in disappointment, about the kind of upbringing they received at home. I believe that people who do their jobs well have one thing in common: They have taken to heart the lessons they learned in childhood, such as:

- Make the most of each moment.
- Don't do to others what you wouldn't want them to do to you.
- Do the best you can under your current circumstances.

These maxims share a common characteristic in that they encourage people to control their behaviour. I believe that having a creed to live by enables people to live governed, but not constricted, by behavioural boundaries. It can even be said that the boundaries our parents teach us will actually set us free.

043: Fights Are Learning Opportunities

Getting into fights is an unavoidable part of growing up. In kindergarten, our children often get into arguments, and the instigators are subjected to strict discipline. When the culprits are brought to the principal's office, they are usually crying and it takes a long time to calm them down. They are sobbing so much that they cannot talk and do not understand that what they did was wrong. I take whatever time is needed to talk to them about their problems.

On the other hand, these incidents provide an opportunity for the victims of fights or bullying to learn to calm themselves down and resolve their problems. It is not enough to simply run away from something unpleasant; they need to know that there is a small spark of positivity in every experience, and we have an obligation to provide that meaning.

When my daughter was in elementary school, she had a particularly rambunctious boy for a classmate. One day, she came home complaining that he had bullied her. The first thing I did was tell her that it wasn't the end of the world. After all, she had learned something (i.e. that she didn't like whatever it was the boy had done to her), hadn't she? If she didn't like it, then it was likely that other people would not like it if she did the same thing to them, so she had learned a valuable lesson.

"If something is so bad that you can't stand it anymore, tell your teacher," I said. "And if you can't do that, tell me and I will pass the message along."

Except in extreme cases where fights or bullying results in injury, start by expressing understanding towards the child's fear and discomfort. Then, help him or her take the first steps towards reconciling the issue within his or her own mind.

We see all sorts of children in kindergarten. There are, of course, repeat troublemakers, and I get the feeling that their constant misbehaviour is caused by background issues that lie not with the children themselves, but with their families who fail to properly address their children's circumstances.

Encourage children to think about what these situations mean. It will benefit those on both sides of the equation. In victims, it nurtures a healthy dislike for bullying and helps teach them that they should not do those things to others, thus stopping a potential cycle of violence. Meanwhile, perpetrators learn as they apologise, acknowledging that what they did was wrong, clearly delineating the line between good and bad.

In this way, the parents of young children should use their kids' fights as an opportunity for children and grown-ups alike to seek positive outcomes from the experience and to learn lessons inside the bad situations.

Some parents are quick to complain ("How could you let this happen to my child?") when their child is in a fight or is bullied. But getting angry achieves nothing, and it is liable to damage relationships between parents. Any discussion among involved parties should seek to identify some kind of positive takeaway.

It appears to me that some parents view their children as possessions, and their anger at children's fights or bullying stems from their misguided idea that their "property" has been damaged in some way. Children are not chattels; they are people, and the ideas we instil in them now will become deeply ingrained attitudes when they grow up.

I think that we need to take every opportunity to teach our children lessons that will help them make their way through life and remember that our children are watching the ways in which grown-ups deal with and seek solutions to difficult situations.

044: Selfish People Must Lead Awful Lives

Viktor Frankl was a Jewish psychiatrist who survived the Nazi concentration camps. His book, *Man's Search for Meaning*, had a profound effect on me. He believed that life was significant, even under the most trying circumstances. Even when it seems that you have lost everything, you may at least have someone or something awaiting your return, so there is always something that you can do for another. In that sense, people are contributing to society simply by being alive.

Frankl witnessed many facets of human life in the concentration camps. He wrote that he clearly witnessed the sublime nature of the human spirit in people who were about to be executed and still found it within them to share their bread with others, and in those who were literally dying of disease but still found the energy to offer a kind word to those suffering around them. This empathy towards others is unique to the human spirit.

Life is made richer by one's proximity to others. When those around us are happy, we cannot help but become happy ourselves. Conversely, a purely selfish life is worthless. People cannot live alone. The same goes for children: Parents may think that they are alone as they raise their children, but the truth is different. We must not forget that our children grow up thanks to the effort of the people and community around us. We must keep others in mind when we raise our children and teach our young that life is a series of relationships and interactions with other people.

That is why kindergarten education places such significance on collectivity. By sharing in activities and making things with their friends, children develop a feeling of togetherness. The role of kindergarten and elementary school is to teach children these lessons.

045: Parents Need to Experience More

Many parents are keen to give their children a wide range of experiences, but do not immediately see the value of broadening their own experiences.

In kindergarten, our children take violin lessons, and sometimes one mother or another will comment on how our kindergarten would be ideal were it not for the violin classes. I guess they think that the violin is snobby, but I believe that the violin lessons are no different than playing in the sandpit; obviously not every child is going to become a professional violinist, but that is not the point of these lessons anyway. There are two reasons why we have violin lessons in kindergarten. The first is to expose children to a common international language (i.e. music and music notation). The second is to make children use their brains and their hands and to develop their ability to recognise harmony and disharmony. The ability to differentiate between "comfortable" and "uncomfortable" sounds is useful in many facets of life. In fact, I was pleasantly surprised to discover that children were able to concentrate much better in other kindergarten activities after taking violin lessons, not to mention the fact that their ability to sing as a chorus improved, as well.

It is difficult to convince parents to make their children participate in some activity that the parents themselves have never experienced. If a parent sees no point in violin lessons, it is likely that this attitude will rub off on their children. It disappoints me that some parents see no need for their children to experience things that they themselves had never experienced. How can you tell that discovering and learning the violin will not change your child's life? Music, like English, is a common global language; do-re-mi is do-re-mi wherever you go. Any child who cannot read music and is comfortable handling musical instruments will be able to interact and communicate with people from all around the world at the drop of a hat. How could you wish to deny your child a chance at doing something so wonderful?

I always tell my staff that if they are unsure of whether or not to attempt something, to just do it, even if only to avoid the need to think up excuses for not doing it. The quickest way to increase your child's breadth of experience is to increase your own. The important point is not whether you are good or bad at any particular activity, but rather that you express a positive interest in a variety of things.

I remember some people kicked up a similar fuss when we introduced computers in kindergarten for the children to draw pictures on. That was almost 20 years ago when computers were still expensive and had yet to be introduced to elementary schools, let alone kindergartens. Some people back then questioned the need for computers in a kindergarten. But, not even five years later, we were vindicated when computers were being introduced en masse to elementary schools as part of the informational studies curriculum. There will always be parents who complain about this and that, saying things such as, "You don't need all that fancy stuff in kindergarten," and "It's too early to expose kids to that kind of thing." But denying your child the opportunity to try something just because you don't know about it or cannot do it yourself serves only to strangle their potential. Parents can broaden their children's horizons by expanding their own experience.

046: When Children Test the Boundaries

Children are always testing the boundaries of their parents' patience. Just as boxers test each other's limits in the early rounds of a fight with explorative jabs, children are constantly engaging in mischief to determine just how much grown-ups will put up with. At times, they will deliberately do something naughty just to see how much they can get away with. In other words, they want to test the limits of what parents, teachers, and other grown-ups will permit.

That is why, when you discipline your children, you must be thorough. I ask my teachers in kindergarten to provide a clear line between acceptable and unacceptable behaviour through strict discipline. If you genuinely hope your children will grow up to be people who do not trouble others, you will discipline them seriously when necessary. If you do not, the children themselves will ultimately suffer. That is why I believe that it is important for the grown-ups closest to each child (for example the parents and grandparents) to praise and discipline children rather than leaving it up to the community at large.

Once children learn to stand up and then reach the age of two, they often knock things over on the tables that they have just learned how to reach. They are testing the boundaries of their parents' patience. These are ideal opportunities to set behavioural limits through tough discipline to show them that we don't always get what we want in life. Therefore, don't be afraid to give your child a strict telling off in this type of situation.

Specific methods of discipline will vary from family to family. Perhaps you prefer to start with a firm but patient admonishment, saying things such as, "If you knock something over, stand it up again," or "What do you say when you have done something naughty?" If that doesn't achieve the desired result, feel free to raise your voice or give your child a smack. Whatever your preferred method of discipline, recognise that these situations are the ideal time to scold your child and really mean it. The important thing is that you recognise when your child is testing the boundaries and use the opportunity to show him or her the clear limits of behaviour that you are willing to tolerate.

047: Children as Citizens

Have you ever thought about why we discipline our children?

Parents have an innate ability to recognise opportunities to discipline their children. It's quite fascinating. Let's say, for example, that you tell your children never to run onto the road without first checking to see that it is clear of traffic. Why do you do this? At first glance, you might think that it was because of the potentially fatal risk of being run over.

That is of course valid, but it is merely a personal reason. The real reason we discipline our children is because we do not want them to create trouble for others. Like it or not, children are members of society, so we tell them off at times when it appears that they have forgotten to behave in socially appropriate ways.

When my boys were young, they played baseball. One of them was a catcher and I often told him that he must take extra care to avoid accidents and injuries because he was responsible for an important position on the team, and that the whole team would suffer if he got injured and could no longer play. One time, when he was in fifth grade, he accidentally cut his hand with a Stanley knife during crafts class. They took him to the hospital, and I arrived just as the doctor began stitching him up. I could hear my boy wailing from outside the surgery room, but as soon as I opened the door and walked in, he became quiet and began to apologise. As I urged him to be more careful in the future, I reminded him that this kind of injury affected others and that the repercussions would be felt by those people which included his teammates and his teachers.

Children are a part of society and must eventually grow up to become independent members of the community. With that future in mind, I believe that we should discipline our children so that they will grow into adults who contribute, rather than take away from, the collective good.

048: "Living Your Own Life" Is Nonsense

We often hear people talking about "living your own life." What on earth does that mean, *living your own life*? If everybody in society did only as they pleased, life would soon devolve into a chaos of self-centredness. Everything we do should be appropriate for the time, place, and occasion, and individuality is no exception. "Being your own person" is fine as long as it is appropriate for the situation.

I believe the modern preoccupation for "finding yourself" and "living your own life" is a manifestation of a lack of confidence. In fact, studies have repeatedly shown that we Japanese people do not see ourselves as useful individuals. We tend to have low opinions of ourselves and are likely to be insecure. I believe that this is because there is no opportunity to experience a sense of achievement during early childhood.

Self-affirmation comes from having your accomplishments recognised and praised during childhood.

Recently, one of my sons, now a university student, announced that he was going overseas with two older students during spring vacation. "Good for you," I said. "It's great that you are turning your attention to the world and thinking about going to foreign climes."

My boy was strangely silent, so I asked him if anything was wrong. "I don't get it," he said. "Are you praising me?"

"Of course I am. What's wrong with that?"

"Nothing. That's good to hear," he mumbled, and I reflected that perhaps I had been a little hard on him recently.

This incident reminded me of how children develop their sense of self-affirmation. A few weeks later, I was on his case again for getting his priorities wrong. I had asked him to look after things at home as I was about to leave on an overseas business trip, and he said that he couldn't because he would be away at camp with his extracurricular group. I guess a delicate mix of praise and discipline is necessary when raising children, and we just have to hope to get the balance right.

To develop your child's self-affirmation, you must expose them to a sense of achievement and praise. Parental praise reinforces good behaviour in children. Ideally, you will praise your children in a way that makes them feel that they are making a useful contribution.

In kindergarten, we place a premium on group activities that involve self-expression, such as class choirs. When everybody makes an effort towards a collective goal, we shower them in praise for their success. We tell them things like, "The whole audience loved the way you all sang together," That's what you can achieve when you work as a group," "Your long-term efforts have now paid off," and "Well done, all of you."

At home, be sure to voice your recognition of your children's ongoing efforts, whether it involves doing their chores, extracurricular lessons, or even just playing. By providing them with a sense of achievement from a young age and reinforcing those successes with praise, you develop your children's sense of self-affirmation, and in doing so, enable them to live their own lives in the true sense of the word without having to constantly seek affirmation elsewhere.

049: Hooray for Child Rearing!

Child rearing is the process by which we raise our children from their exclusively private world to become members of public society. It is our role as parents and families to teach our children to become independent so that they can survive out in the big, wide world. They cannot hide behind mother's apron forever.

Once upon a time, we had strong communities and our parents felt safe in leaving children under the watchful eye of neighbours. Homes were often packed with extended family members such as grandparents who generally lived with the family, so children grew up inside large communities. In that sense, children were much more "socialised" than they are today. Now, in the age of the nuclear family, mothers find themselves isolated in their parenting roles. The troubles and worries of raising children fall entirely on their shoulders, and with no one to advise them and no idea of what to do, parents wind up abusing their children out of frustration.

I urge all parents to remember that children one day must become adult members of society and, therefore, the act of parenting is, in and of itself, a great service to the community. Unfortunately, many parents fail to recognise their gift to society.

I was brought up to believe that a person's life was only complete when we had grown up, married, raised children, and been blessed with grandchildren. I think that we are a part of a grand circle of life, so it is my duty to play my part and keep the cycle going on to subsequent generations. Japan's future is in peril if today's youths are unaware of their position in the grand scheme of things. When lives are devoted to finding a dream job or spent engrossed in hobbies while having children is reduced to a digression, Japan's downfall is surely near.

Raising children is a person's ultimate contribution to society, and a vital part of ensuring the continuance of communities, societies, and entire nations. Notwithstanding expectations on how children should be raised, you are doing a wonderful thing by rearing children in the first place.

050: Rejoicing in Tomorrow

What is happiness?

I still read books to, or rather, with my daughter. Once, we were reading a biography of Socrates, and in one scene, he asked some youths in the street, "What does happiness mean to you?" I took the opportunity to ask my daughter what she thought happiness was, and she replied that she didn't know. We read on and came to a scene where Socrates said, "I don't know what happiness is," which made my daughter cheer in delight. It seems that happiness is too difficult of a problem even for Socrates to solve.

It may make us happy to have our dreams come true, but if we become obsessed with achieving our dreams, we begin to lose sight of happiness altogether. I am happy just being with my children, and even reading picture books to them brings me joy. I guess happiness is found in these everyday aspects of life, yet human nature will not allow us to revel in these joys despite their proximity. We rarely recognise what we have until it is lost.

It is not unheard of for residents of my facility, for people with special needs, to be in good spirits at dinner, but dead the next morning. Dealing with these realities on a daily basis teaches us to be thankful for tomorrow. It is the dawn of another day, and you are alive to enjoy it… now *that* is happiness.

Perhaps happiness is being able to talk to children about things that will inspire dreams and aspirations in their futures, and all of us living a positive life in the hope of moving forward in a common direction. It pleases me to no end to tell our children that tomorrow will be better than today.

In Conclusion

I cannot remember when I decided to become a teacher, but I guess it was around the first grade when I discovered a book that provided a gentle introduction to the world of *kanji* characters that I had a vague idea that I wanted to be a Japanese teacher when I grew up. Later in life, my English teacher in my high school and a pedagogy lecturer at university made a great impact on me. Now, I am the principal of a kindergarten and the director of a nursery school and a facility for people with special needs. I am very much involved in the world of education, but not as a Japanese teacher; however, I guess at least part of my dream came true.

The idea for this book came while lecturing at university. I wanted to take a clinical look at education practices and offer answers to the issues of parenting that I have developed through my experience of raising three children and observing many children, staff members, and parents in the course of my work.

Education practitioners are required to incorporate a range of perspectives into our work, including clinical pedagogy, educational administration, and developmental psychology. They are also required to seek solutions to a myriad of problems. We must "connect the dots," as it were, and link all of these approaches.

Meanwhile, at home, parents should enjoy their lives and show their children how to come to terms with society and achieve personal growth. Seeing their parents strive for personal growth is the ultimate inspiration for children. To that end, I think that it is vital to develop a new perspective when we become parents and to strike a positive balance between who we were before and after having children.

Children who can behave with consideration for others rather than selfishly will ultimately lead a better, richer life. The best way to ensure your children grow up to be productive, considerate people is to lead by example. Show them how to be the people you want them to be.

These days, we often hear of people complaining about the noise of their local nursery school. Similarly, there are more cases where people who have been blessed with children end up abusing them. This is sad beyond words. We live in an age where everybody is looking for convenience, but seeking efficiency and convenience in child raising only results in an unhappy child-hood and trouble for the community.

Children are our future and the treasures of society as a whole. They grow up under the protection of their parents, under the nurturing care of their kindergarten, nursery school, and schoolteachers, and with the assistance of the whole community. Parents should therefore realise that raising children is taking the time to nurture treasures on behalf of society.

Parents tend to try too hard to "make" their children more mature, but there is no need for that. Children have an innate ability to learn; they grow by watching their parents, their friends, and their teachers. However, this only works when their parents provide them with correct examples of how to live properly to achieve growth.

In conclusion, I think that the very basis of child raising is to create a cycle of happiness based on learning and growth: When parents learn, children develop.

Dr. Hanns Stekel

The Japan Project of the Johann Sebastian Bach Music School in Vienna

In 2005, the Johann Sebastian Bach Music School in Vienna (JSBM) had been in existence for five years. During this time, the JSBM youth orchestra travelled to Japan with the support of the Music School in Wiener Neustadt, Austria. Its destination was Utsunomiya, the capital city of the Tochigi Prefecture.

One of the hosts of this cultural exchange tour was Tatsuo Yamamura, the Director of the Makoto Kindergarten and the social service foundation "AIAIKAI," which operates a facility for the handicapped (Heartfield) and a day care centre (Heartfull) in addition to the kindergarten.

Most of the participating young musicians and teachers from Austria were in Japan for the first time. Accommodation in guest families and direct cooperation with schools, communities, and organisers in the area enabled us to get to know the country very quickly. Japan made a deep impression on us, and through concerts and other musical activities, we experienced cultural exchange in the truest sense.

At the end of the tour, while we were still in Japan, ideas already began to emerge of how we might be able to continue this cooperation.

The Project

Only one year after the tour of the youth orchestra, a proposal for a joint project had been drawn up and approved.

The Makoto Kindergarten was to be the focal point. It was a large facility with around 350 children between the ages of three to five years old. Children there would receive music lessons in large groups (of about 15), which would be conducted in accordance with the principles of early music education, but would also include violin lessons.[1] For this, an appropriate number of violins were purchased and the first course began in September 2006.

Each year, two teachers were selected and given orientation by the JSBM and were then sent to Japan. Instruction was conducted in English. The aim was to combine the European know-how of violin teachers from Austria with the teaching methods of a Japanese kindergarten. In addition, in order to also establish a music school structure based on a European model, violin instruction was also offered in the afternoons to outsiders and children who had finished kindergarten. This was a completely new idea in Utsunomiya which aroused great interest from the very beginning. Both institutions were able to organise the financing, for which the Japanese partner assumed responsibility for the major part.

The project developed very well in the following years. A high point was achieved in the summer of 2010 with a successful big concert in Utsunomiya. The catastrophic earthquake and tsunami in Fukushima on 11 March 2011 brought everything to an abrupt end. With the help of the Diakonie in Vienna, the project director Tatsuo Yamamura himself organised emergency measures in the affected area.

After this, the system of early music education with violin instruction was continued in a reduced form with Japanese teachers. This has continued until the present day, but both sides hope that it will soon be possible to bring the full project back to life again.

Project Challenges and Experiences

From the very beginning, the teachers from Europe were faced with many challenges. It was necessary to adjust to Japanese ways of doing things in both daily life and at work; cultural and language differences were hurdles that had to be overcome. All of the instructors were trained violin teachers, most of whom had experience in Europe with early music education and had worked with groups, but not with kindergarten children. The methods

---

1   The method decided upon was "Colourstrings" developed by Géza and Csaba Szilvay. Those applying for teaching positions would have to have appropriate knowledge of this approach.

they had learned had to be adapted to the age of the pupils and to Japanese conditions.

Paul Mittermayer was a teacher in the first year of the project and then, after a rather long pause, returned to it. He drew up the curriculum for the project and with good organisation, he established an excellent foundation for all of the other violin teachers.

He describes his experience as follows:

"In the JSBM project in Utsunomiya, Japan, I had a unique opportunity to go to a foreign country and to gain exceptional professional and personal experience.

Looking back on the project and thinking about the effect it had on me, I am reminded somewhat of the medieval "Walz," the journeymen's years of wandering from workshop to workshop, once they had finished their training. For good reason, this was for centuries the prerequisite for being allowed to take the master craftsman's examination of the guilds. In this way, the journeymen learned new methods of craftsmanship, as well as gained experience in living in new places and working with different people.

There are things about life that cannot be learned from books, that other people cannot tell you, that cannot be seen in pictures. They can only be experienced first hand, in actual situations, because they involve direct contact between people in unaccustomed or even foreign contexts.

And the context of this project on the other side of the world was certainly both foreign and unaccustomed – in some respects you could even say it was daring. By this, I naturally don't mean the external living conditions, but the cold water into which one is thrown when obliged to teach in a way that would be simply rejected with a "no thanks" in one's home country. But this "no thanks" would have been based on a premature judgement stemming from one's own limited experience, incomplete knowledge, and preconceived ideas that are never universal.

My colleague Stefan Gröger and I were sent to Utsunomiya as violin teachers in this JSBM project, with the task of getting the instrumental instruction started. And as mentioned above, we found ourselves in an unexpected situation – even in one that we previously would not have dared to undertake. Who in Austria would set out to give all the children in a kindergarten over the age of four to five violin lessons? Who would dare to do this in groups? Is it possible to imagine only having violins in the classes and not being able to practice at home? Who here would dare to let foreigners who don't know the local language give instruction?

In Austria, this would have been "mission impossible" for me. But we were there and had work to do.

The form of instruction was the result of organisational, financial, and also social conditions, as we knew. Our main goal for the moment was not to bring individual children to the highest level of mastery on the violin – this was seen as a possibility for the future – but first of all to give all the children the opportunity to hold the instrument in their hands and learn basic musical skills. And, moreover, to be able to do this with teachers from Central Europe, the cradle of European classical music, which was clearly an attractive prospect. This experience and their first little concerts on the violin should be something that the children would never forget, as was clearly explained to us.

Those children who wanted to continue to play the violin after they finished kindergarten or elementary school could take one-to-one lessons, in what would initially be a small European-style music school.

Throughout their entire musical lives, violinists and violin teachers are oriented towards achieving as high a standard of playing as possible. Thus, it is a big challenge to lower one's standards and make necessary compromises that specific circumstances demand.

More difficult than accepting objective external circumstances is being able to think outside the box of one's own mindset and to transcend the social conditioning to which one has been subjected by one's environment. You can understand that things are different in different places – to put it rather mundanely; you can accept this, but it is difficult to actually live with it. There are many differences, large and small, in interpersonal relations and in working together that can easily lead to misunderstandings or simply to both sides failing to understand each other.

My native Japanese wife was a big help to me in learning how to distinguish between what was dictated by custom and what stemmed from individual personalities. This made it easier for me to correctly interpret situations.

I would like to mention only two considerable cultural differences here: the relationship between the group and the individual, and the interpretation of what people say.

Simply put, one could say that whereas in our society the smallest social unit is the individual, in Japan it is the group. In Europe, a group is the sum of all the individuals in it; in Japan, the individual is defined by his or her role in the group. The relation between an individual's personal needs and the goals of the group is seen in a different light, and the kind of balance desired is different. In brief, in Japan, one often feels that it is better not to assert oneself too much.

In Japan, nuances in language play a more important role than they do in Europe. There, one is expected to exert great effort to understand what is said, whereas in Europe, those speaking bear the responsibility of expressing themselves clearly.

Japan: Please try to understand me!

Europe: Tell me what you want!

We Europeans are less sensitive to the small details of spoken language and their significance. But the desire to understand each other and the filter of English – the language in which we usually communicated with each other (along with using our hands) – enabled us to get along.

From the very beginning, we had many opportunities to become acclimated. It was very agreeable that we were immediately included in all activities, parties, and celebrations of the kindergarten, for which we supplied musical accompaniment. When the older children made weekend outings including overnight stays, we went with them and we were regular guests at AIAIKAI, the facility for the handicapped also run by Mr Yamamura, the director of the kindergarten. Every month we gave a small concert there for the patients, and in this way, had further contact with them and their carers. We were invited to weekly soccer games and other types of sports with colleagues of the day care centre, the kindergarten, and AIAIKAI.

As musicians, we often played in Ms. Hara's concerts with pupils and friends.

Great efforts were made to meet our needs, and the first six months went very smoothly. At that point, Stefan left us and was replaced by Nikolay Demerdjev, who became a valued colleague and friend in the next six months.

We very quickly got used to teaching the children. We learned the most important words in Japanese right away: "Mane shite – do what I am doing" was one of the most useful expressions. And this worked very well, as the children there are accustomed to doing things in groups, and we had groups of up to eight children.

We soon had small and large concerts. In April, when the new school year begins, we were happy to have a few pupils who had finished kindergarten to teach on a one-to-one basis in the afternoon. Along with the mothers of the children, to whom group instruction had been offered from the beginning, and the afternoon pupils, we could slowly start making plans for the future. If in one year a tenth of 80–100 children of a kindergarten year continued to learn violin, this would soon lead to a sizable violin class.

Just at this point, when I had the feeling that the seeds we had sown were beginning to develop into little plants, the first year came to an end and I had to leave the project and return to Austria with my family.

If what I have written here does not focus so heavily on teaching, there is a reason for this. It is to be hoped that many children will profit from their experience as little violin pupils. But that is only the obvious and superficial aspect. I personally see a big additional benefit in international understanding, which in times like these should be a very important concern.

It is so essential to get to know other cultures and it is so valuable in this process to also see oneself in the mirror and to recognise one's strengths and weaknesses. It is at times necessary to cut oneself down to size, to withdraw, and not to pass judgement on others on the basis of one's own unquestioned mindset. It is necessary to recognise that there are other ways of doing things, even if one doesn't understand them.

Even though there is no longer any instruction by European teachers in Utsunomiya, the project still has a lasting effect. I myself often realise that I have made hasty criticisms, have looked down on something foreign, and have elevated my own standpoint because I didn't understand something. Then I think back and try to put things in perspective and keep my eyes open.

For the time that I was able to spend in Japan and for the valuable experience that this gave me, I am deeply grateful to those who took the important initiative of bringing this project to life: Mr Yamamura, the Director of the Makoto Kindergarten, and his family; Dr. Stekel, the Director of the JSBM; and Ms. Hara.

I also feel very thankful to the many dear children I was privileged to teach, to the industrious pupils, to my colleagues in the kindergarten for

their friendly reception, and to my fellow violin teachers, Gregor and espe-
cially Nikolay, with whom I have formed a lasting friendship.
   Thank you for the invaluable treasure that has become a part of me, and
something that I can also give to others."
   Nikolay Demerdhziev, violin and viola teacher from Bulgaria, was the
only teacher who stayed two full years in Japan. Along with Paul Mittermayer, he ensured the positive development of the project.
   Here is his summary:
   "To spend a year in a foreign country – that is what I wanted to do in
2007. When I finished my studies at the University of Music and Perform-
ing Arts in Graz, I wanted to go someplace different. It didn't matter where
or how, I simply wanted to get away from Graz and experience something
new. It was in September when I saw in a newspaper that the JSBM was
looking for a violin teacher for a partner school in Japan. The position
was for one year. Without further ado, I applied for the job. The selection
process took place in November, and in January I was informed that my
interview was successful and that I could fly to Japan in March. This was
how my Japanese adventure began.
   Living in a foreign country always involves big adjustments. In my case
it was a professional appointment, but teaching was not the only thing that
I did. I had to spend a lot of time learning Japanese and at least one of the
three alphabets used in Japan. But the language wasn't the only challenge;
there were many other things that are different in Japan. Often these were
quite trivial things, such as turning lights on and off, using restrooms, and
driving a car.
   But back to teaching. Japanese children are very well-behaved and in-
dustrious. This makes it possible to begin teaching them how to play an
instrument much earlier than is the case in Europe. One has to bear in mind
that Japanese children already learn to read and write in kindergarten.
Thus, making violin lessons a required part of the programme of a Japanese
kindergarten is not so surprising. Our European culture is greatly admired
there, and playing the violin is part of this. Children are expected to learn
to appreciate this at an early age.
   That, in Japan, one feels comfortable about being a European, is some-
thing ones notices upon arrival there. But it should never be forgotten

that the Japanese are very proud of their country, and foreign guests are expected to show appropriate respect for Japanese history and culture.

This also applied to the small world of our partner school, where I taught. Learning from each other and working for each other are very important in Japan. The top priorities are not one's own personal interests, but the goals of the project and the children, whose education is the key concern of our Japanese partner in Utsunomiya. The new teachers in the project were told by the director of the kindergarten, "If things go well for your pupils this year, things will also go well for you in Japan!"

I can confirm this from my own experience. After a two-and-a-half year stay in Japan, I have come back to Europe, but I have maintained a very strong attachment to Japan and my colleagues there.

Finally, I would like to say that one should not miss out on the unique opportunity to teach in Japan for a year. If any risk is involved, it is only that after one year, one may not want to leave."

Tatsuo Yamamura
Director in Makoto Kindergarten

The Starting Point in JSBM
-In Purpose of the Person Who Tries to Participate in a Japanese Education System-

Introduction

On September 1st 2007, JSBM Utsunomiya was set up at the Makoto Kindergarten School.

It was a regrettable thing, but the big earthquake which occurred in March 2011 had a great influence on this project.

Teacher dispatch from Vienna has also stopped.

But a Japanese teacher inherits the spirit of this JSBM project, and children also receive music education now.

I feel that it's also significant to describe our thought in time that this project has just concluded.

The purpose of this guide is to help the teachers who come to teach at JSBM and people that are interested in Japanese pre-school education and in this small project that accomplishes different cultural understanding and a cultural exchange through music.

First, I'd like to introduce myself so that you, the reader, can easily understand my position and what I am doing.

Presently I am the principal of the Makoto Kindergarten School. This year (2015) we have approximately 360 students inaugurated. There are three groupings in the kindergarten based on year. There are five first year classes, four second year classes, and four third year classes. Currently we have 50 teachers.

I am also the director of a social welfare foundation called *AIAIKAI*. This has two institutions. One of these institutions, called Heartfield, is a support centre for disabled people. 40 people live at Heartfield, ten people commute from their homes once a day, and three to four people stay temporarily. Heartfield has 46 staff members. The other institution is a nursery called Heartfull Nursery. Infants from the age of zero to five years can attend the nursery. Presently, there are around 70 infants and 30 members of staff.

In the picture on your right, you can see both the Makoto Kindergarten and the Heartfull Nursery. These two institutions are separated by the school grounds.

Besides being the principal of the Makoto Kindergarten School and the director of both Heartfield and the Heartfull Nursery, I also take part in coaching university students who want to acquire their teaching license. On top of this, in association with the police, I attend conferences to provide advice to primary and secondary schools.

Moreover, some years ago, I worked as a primary and secondary school counsellor for approximately five years.

I have a wide range of experience concerning the education and development of not just school children from an early age through to students of university age, but disabled people as well.

If you add the number of staff members at all three institutions mentioned above, the number exceeds 100.

While I am the manager of these institutions, I am also an education researcher. The contents of this guide are written from both points of view.

I: The Purpose of the Project

On September 25th 2007, there was a ceremony where the education and international cultural exchange declaration was signed. The contents of the declaration are written below.

The Makoto Kindergarten in Utsunomiya Japan and the JSBM have agreed to form a deep friendship so that culture and education can be exchanged and the children can broaden their horizons.

Based on this declaration, The Makoto Kindergarten and the JSBM will exchange education and culture in the hope that the children attending the respective schools can become friends and develop the international relationship we have.

The declaration is written in both German and Japanese, and each school has a copy.

On September 25th 2008, the principle of the Makoto Kindergarten and the principle of the JSBM signed the declaration. This was witnessed by MMag. Michael Bubik.

II: The Aim of the Project

The JSBM-Vienna principal Hans Stekel and I consulted and confirmed the goals of this project from our respective points of view. We confirmed four things:

1) JSBM-Vienna, through musical knowledge and ensemble, aims to promote the talent of each individual child.
2) The children who learn how to play European instruments will be educated by the Austria music education system.
3) In the class, the teachers will use English. By using English, the children will be exposed to a foreign language.
4) Through exchange students, collaborations, and seminars, we endeavour to promote the relationship between Japan and Austria.

III: JSBM-Utsunomiya Basic Policy

To realise these aims, JSBM Utsunomiya was established. JSBM Utsunomiya's basic policy is written down in a document that was distributed during the declaration ceremony. This document is very important and has been written in both Japanese and English.

The project of creating the JSBM-Utsunomiya was enabled by the cooperation between the schools involved in Austria and Japan.

The implementation of this project involved putting a part of the music education system of Vienna into the educational system of a Japanese kindergarten. This was achieved with the help of an experienced teacher from Austria. While all of the children can have the valuable experience of a musical education, this program also enables the educators to find especially musically talented children at a young age and to start their development early, thus giving them time to learn without having to rush them.

Teaching children the language of music is also helpful in aiding their human and social development. When children at an early age receive music classes as a normal part of their education, it helps them to accept and identify with music at later ages and encourages them to learn to actively.

We also wish to carry out this program at the music school in Utsunomiya in order to further the cultural exchange between Japan and Austria.

IV: JSBM-Utsunomiya. The Present Situation

I will explain the project from four different points of view:

1) Man
2) Materials
3) Money
4) Management

IV-(1): Teacher and Students

Regarding (1), I must make the aspects of both the teacher and the students clear. Regarding the teachers, JSBM-Vienna interviews the prospective teachers and dispatches them to Utsunomiya. Of course there are many matters to be resolved but these can be worked out.

The teachers who are dispatched to Utsunomiya belong to an organisation. They need to be aware that they will be teaching in a country that has a totally different culture. Although the aim of this project is to introduce the Austrian musical system, it needs to be adapted to suit the different culture. The teacher's character is the most important factor. On top of this, leadership and the ability to educate are important for success.

The reliance between the children and the parents and the kindergarten staff is also important. This reliance is also related to how the teacher performs.

The teacher exists for the students and not the other way around. This is a precondition of being a teacher.

Another important factor is the student. If JSBM-Utsunomiya was established independently, it would have financial difficulties because it wouldn't have the appropriate financial backing.

The reality is that many parents in this area hesitate to allow their children to learn how to play the violin because a musical environment hasn't been established yet. However, the number of people interested in classical music has risen recently. This is due to the influence of the media. Even though interest has risen, the management of a philharmonic orchestra is difficult because there aren't sufficient funds. The philharmonic orchestra tried to spread the interest in classical music by visiting schools but many people are worried that traditional Japanese culture is at threat.

IV-(2): The Type of Student at JSBM-Utsunomiya

JSBM-Utsunomiya's students can be divided into three types:

1) Kinder: Children who are four/five years old.
2) Parents: Parents of the children who attend the kindergarten.
3) JSBM: Primary school students, junior high school students, high school students, and general members of the public.

From the table, you can see that the children who attend the kindergarten are enjoying the violin performances the most.

The idea of introducing the Vienna system is a very important factor to promote this project because the children can spread their experiences. This should increase the number of people interested in music.

It is my hope that by allowing the children to become familiar with musical instruments such as the violin, the cello, and the viola, the children will be able to broaden their horizons and strengthen their character.

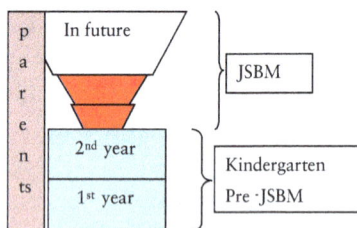

Moreover, it is easy to gain trust when the kindergarten education system acts as a mediator between JSBM-Utsunomiya and the community. Making classical music more familiar for people in the community is important.

Parents who wish to learn the violin have a very important role in spreading the fantastic reputation that JSBM-Utsunomiya has to other parents.

In 2007, eight out of 55 of the five-year-olds who graduated from the kindergarten joined JSBM-Utsunomiya. At the present time, we predict that this will increase year after year. From now on, we need to think about how to make it possible for primary school students to continue studying. On top of this, we want to recruit junior high school students. Adolescence can be a difficult experience. However, junior high school students can benefit from being taught music.

IV-(3): The Education System Before Attending School in Japan

Children can choose from two courses before attending school. One is the kindergarten course. When the children become three years old, they can attend kindergarten. By law, kindergartens are part of the same system as primary schools, junior high schools, high schools, and universities. Therefore, the way to teach kindergarten is restricted and requires a smooth transition between the respective schools. Of course, the kindergarten teachers need to have graduated from university and have a teaching license.

The other day, I visited Austria and observed a kindergarten class for a short period of time. I was surprised to know that the director wanted his kindergarten to be more like the kindergartens in Japan.

The other course is the nursery course. This system is part of the welfare system. Infants can attend the nursery from zero to five years old. The infants who attend the nursery can stay there longer than the children attending the kindergarten. Nurseries do not have long vacations.

In summary, the children can enter the nursery from zero years of age. When the child becomes three years old, they become a part of the education system and they enter kindergarten.

IV-(4): How Parents Think of Their Children's Education Before Attending Primary School

We can see from the research that one of the main reasons why people want their children to attend the kindergarten is because their children are exposed to a wide variety of experiences. With this kind of background, we are carrying out explanatory meetings. From 2011, all of the four- and five-year-old students will have lessons at JSBM-Utsunomiya.

V: Education Information

Regarding the contents, we basically use the 'colour strings' method. This was used by the first teacher, Paul Mittermyer. However, from a practical point of view, there is an issue that should be solved by the teacher. The comments that Paul Mittermyer made when we performed live on Tochigi radio are included below.

"At the kindergarten, we start in groups with four year-old children. At this age, we have to establish the basics of making music. The children have to learn to listen not just to themselves but also to the others. They have to learn to wait for each other and to react to each other. They have to learn to imagine sounds, how to deal with an instrument, and many other things. This is elementary musical education.

And of course we try to give them an idea of what it means to play the violin. Learning to play the violin is not easy and not every child is interested in playing the violin. However, all children should be able to play a little music with easy elements and feel what it is like to play music together. From this point, they can decide if they are really interested and go on to play more.

The 'colour string' method of Geza Silvay is a good basic method because the children can understand it easily and it is fun to play using these notes. They have already started to learn to read notes and as a result, it is very easy and natural. Moreover, this method improves the quality of bowing and prepares the left hand very well. As a result, the children who go on playing the violin after they have graduated from the kindergarten have very good basics. We don't want the children to play very complicated things but we want to give them good basics.

With the JSBM pupils who have graduated from the kindergarten, we can go on with this method. With older children, we choose an individual program from conventional music books."

When I implemented Vienna's music education system, I modified the original form to suit the Japanese educational system. Even though we are both private kindergarten schools, the place where this project is being carried out is completely different.

I have implemented Vienna's system as a part of our curriculum, which means that it is officially recognised. JSBM-Utsunomiya was established on the premises of the kindergarten. Children at the kindergarten study at JSBM-Utsunomiya as well. Therefore, JSBM-Utsunomiya needs to cooperate with the staff at the kindergarten. After all, teaching is to help the children grow and encourage talents that the children have.

In the learning process, teachers need to pay particular attention to the trust that exists between the teacher and the students, the way to communicate to the children, the child's experiences, and the child's life. Understanding that this is central to teaching is the job of the teacher. Understanding not just the central aspects of education, but other surrounding aspects of education is also important because understanding the surrounding aspects of education has a direct effect on how the teacher supports the children. However, not ever child needs this special attention.

V-(2): *The Theory of the Teacher and the Theory of the Learner*

My colleagues in Europe and I often talk about whether or not the children we teach are interested in learning to play the violin. Making children who are not interested play the violin is a waste of time for both the teachers and the children. This thought is based on motivation theory, especially intrinsic motivation theory.

I am not going to support this theory at the kindergarten level. I'd like to illustrate my point by using an example that looks at a child who needs to learn sign language in order to communicate. Not teaching sign language until the child wants to learn it is not practical or acceptable in education. In society, there are handicapped people and people who aren't handicapped. Society needs children to become good citizens. Whether the child wants to learn sign language or not isn't the point. In order to become a good citizen, they must learn how to communicate.

Of course educational contents need to be selected carefully according to the child's stage of development, because as basic policy of this project shows, to provide an opportunity to learn the violin will contribute to the formation of the child's personality. Playing instruments and studying from a foreign teacher are necessary for the children to grow.

I think that the most important thing in the field of kindergarten education is to stimulate the student's intellectual curiosity. This idea is based on learner's theory. Based on this idea, the students should start wanting to study for themselves. Studying with other students is effective because students can raise the quality of their learning by influencing each other. This kind of learning is mirror learning.

Another important question that needs to be addressed is how to make a good learning atmosphere. I expect the teachers to be dedicated and work to the best of their abilities.

VI: Finance

The issues concerning finance are comparatively well solved because we have the kindergarten. Originally I wanted JSBM-Utsunomiya to be managed independently. In order to do this, we would have to solve some complex issues. For example, we would have to solve the problem of how to gather students. Even in Japan, so-called private music schools are very common and widespread. Furthermore, because there is a lot of competition, it is difficult to get students. In strict financial conditions, we need to provide instruments and children accidently drop the instruments, so we need to think about how to make money for repairs and to purchase things like textbooks.

VII: Management

Concerning management, the issue is the number of years that dispatched teachers are going to stay. On top of this, there is another issue. This concerns the teacher's motivation toward the project and the teacher's ability. The teachers who take part in this project must always be forward looking and attempt to improve their ability as a teacher.

Of course the kindergarten staff and teachers will support the dispatched teachers. It goes without saying that cooperation between JSBM-Utsunomiya's teachers and the staff at the kindergarten is important.

From now on, I'd like to find the words to express JSBM-Utsunomiya's philosophy and I'm looking for practical activities for JSBM-Utsunomiya. Up until now, the following lessons, concerts, and seminars have taken place.

In a knot.

I'm different culture time, and it's a difficult thing to get over the difference as the Japanese Bunka and the European Bunka and make music education in infancy be formed above all, but I'm thinking it's worth challenging sufficiently.

The key is in the following points.

1. Suggest teacher's European understanding about Japanese culture and an education system.
2. The teacher dispatched from Vienna adapts himself or herself to Japanese culture and the situation. The teacher also has the spirit in which the study which develops education technique is eager.

www.ingramcontent.com/pod-product-compliance
Lightning Source LLC
Chambersburg PA
CBHW062043270326
41929CB00014B/2527